C. S. Lewis: Defender of the Faith

C. S. LEWIS

Defender of the Faith

by
Richard B. Cunningham

WIPF & STOCK · Eugene, Oregon

Wipf and Stock Publishers
199 W 8th Ave, Suite 3
Eugene, OR 97401

C. S. Lewis: Defender of the Faith
By Cunningham, Richard B.
Copyright©1967 by Cunningham, Richard B.
ISBN 13: 978-1-55635-922-4
Publication date 3/26/2008
Previously published by Westminster Press, 1967

To My Father and Mother
from whom I first heard the Good News

Series Foreword

C. S. Lewis (1898–1963) taught Medieval and Renaissance Language and Literature at Oxford and Cambridge Universities for almost four decades.

He wrote much for publication: literary criticism, poetry, theology, spirituality, science fiction, juvenile literature, novels, autobiography, but alas no plays. Over and above that, he kept up a fierce correspondence for decades; 3,228 letters of his compiled and edited by Walter Hooper have been published in three volumes (2000–2006).

Hooper, long the literary adviser to the Estate of C. S. Lewis, has done much of the primal research on Lewis, editing and seeing to publication perhaps a dozen collections of Lewis's shorter writings (essays, articles, addresses; literary criticism; diaries).

Most Lewis books are still in print in one way or another. But various studies of and commentaries on Lewisiana by others have not had the same longevity. Many are now out of print, but there is much research and review yet to be done.

To aid present and future scholars, Wipf and Stock Publishers has established a series devoted to worthy books on or about Lewis. Perhaps because I have done four books on or about Lewis, Wipf and Stock has asked me to be the general editor of the series.

William Griffin
Series Editor for C. S. Lewis Studies
2007

CONTENTS

Preface	11
I. THE APOLOGIST	13
The Nature and Purpose of Apologetics	18
C. S. Lewis: The Man and the Author	21
II. THE APOLOGETIC SCENE	33
The World as It Ought to Be	33
Our Radical New Era	36
The Areas of Change	36
Chronological Snobbery	38
Twentieth-Century Naturalism	41
The Abolition of Man	42
The Major Abolitionist: Modern Science	45
Natural Science	46
Psychology	50
Philosophy	53
The Present Stage of Abolition: Mass Conformity	55
Education	55
Government, Economics, and News Media	57
Society	59
The Post-Christian Era	62
An Appraisal of Lewis' World View	65

III. The Foundation of Apologetics — 67
Epistemology: The Problem of Knowledge — 67
The Origin and History of Language — 70
Imagination: The Organ of Meaning — 73
Mythology: Grasping the Nonconceptual — 74
Metaphor: Supplying the Tools of Reason — 75
Reason: The Organ of Truth — 77
Faith and Knowledge — 80
Hermeneutics: The Science of Biblical Interpretation — 84
General Principles — 84
Transposition — 84
Revelation — 87
Inspiration — 88
Biblical Criticism — 91
Biblical Mythology and Metaphorical Language — 94
Theology: The Formulation of Faith — 102
The Doctrine of God — 103
Time and Eternity — 106
The Doctrine of the Trinity — 107
The Person and Work of Christ — 109
Man and Sin — 111
Salvation — 114
The Church and the Sacraments — 116
The Christian Life — 118
Eschatology — 124
Devils and Angels — 124
Hell — 125
Heaven — 127
Purgatory — 128
The Resurrection of the Body — 129
The Second Coming — 130
Communication: The Mastery of a Difficult Art — 131

IV. The Apologetic Method — 141
The Literary Forms of Apologetic — 143

CONTENTS

Mythologies	143
Children's Stories	151
Allegory	156
Satire	159
Fantasy	162
Didactic Writings	164
Sermons and Essays	175
Autobiography	178
Devices and Techniques of Debate	179
The Attack	180
Not Strictly Logical	180
Nonlogical Factors in Unbelief	183
The Apologist and His Opponent	187
The Arena of Logic	188
The Defense	191
The Use of Reason	192
The Use of Imagination	194
The Gospel	196
An Evaluation	200

Notes   207

Bibliography   219

PREFACE

DURING MY COLLEGE YEARS, word got around the campus that a series of letters from hell to a junior tempter on earth had fallen into the hands of a British professor of English literature. At a crucial time in my own spiritual experience, when I first began to have intellectual difficulties about the Christian faith, I bought and read *The Screwtape Letters*. Shortly afterward I read *Mere Christianity*. Both books helped me surmount some initial obstacles in my faith. Many years and many books and many changes in thought transpired before I had any further encounter with C. S. Lewis.

When it happened, there was no magnetic force dramatically drawing me back to Lewis — only cold calculation under the compelling necessity of finding a dissertation subject to fulfill a doctoral requirement at Southern Baptist Theological Seminary in Louisville, Kentucky. One day in conversation, Dr. Henlee Barnette suggested to me that a profitable study could be made of C. S. Lewis' method of defending the Christian faith, that he had perhaps been taken too lightly by many theologians. Although familiar with Lewis' literary brilliance, I was quite unaware of the quantity, the diversity, or the real quality of Lewis' writings. Having been preoccupied with reading theology for some years, I myself had never taken Lewis very seriously beyond the college level. At first hesitant, I began to read Lewis again, and the more I read, the more interested I became. The result was my original study, " The Christian

Apologetic of C. S. Lewis," and the current revision for publication, C. S. LEWIS: DEFENDER OF THE FAITH. The farther I have gone, the more convinced I have become that contemporary preachers, theologians, and apologists, as well as laymen, can learn at many points from Lewis about how to defend the Christian faith, including such sticky areas as epistemology and hermeneutics. And I can say, somewhat surprisingly after the long process of writing and rewriting, of digestion and regurgitation, that I am generally more impressed with Lewis than when I began. Though not always persuaded by his logic, I am almost always moved by his spirit.

At the conclusion of writing a book, one realizes that one is indebted to many people. I would be ungrateful not to thank the faculty of Southern Baptist Theological Seminary for having granted me the first annual Teaching Fellowship in the Departments of Theology and Christian Philosophy for 1964–1965. My theological study was enriched by close association with members of my Graduate Committee — Dr. Eric Rust, Dr. Henlee Barnette, Dr. Dale Moody, and Dr. Wayne Ward — men who have been my good friends as well as my professors. I am grateful to Dr. Henlee Barnette for having suggested this subject to me. My greatest intellectual debt is to my former major professor, Dr. Eric Rust, who over a number of years — in the classroom, in seminars, and in personal dialogue — has, for good or ill, taught me more than any other. As for my family, the best word I can give to my wife and children, who have exercised admirable patience for too long, is not so much thanks as the news that the book is finished at last. And, of course, I owe an inestimable debt to C. S. Lewis, a man I have gotten to know though never having been privileged to meet him, who has provided me with some of my richest experiences.

R. B. C.

Albuquerque, New Mexico

I

THE APOLOGIST

NEARLY TWO CENTURIES AGO, Rowland Hill asked, "Why should the Devil have the best tunes?" Too often he does — in the brilliant literary talents of a Swift or Voltaire, a Shaw or Sartre. Too often within the Christian community the artistic ability of the saints is unequal to their piety. But on occasion a Christian adversary arises whose tune is as melodic and exciting as that of the devil's advocates. If Thomas More was right, and "The devill . . . the prowde spirite . . . cannot endure to be mocked," then the diabolical force must have breathed a sigh of relief on November 22, 1963, upon the death of one of its foremost antagonists. That man was Clive Staples Lewis, a quiet, retiring, publicity-shy occupant of the Chair of Medieval and Renaissance Literature at Cambridge University. Lewis' fame was based on diversified accomplishments — as a foremost literary critic, a famed Medieval and Renaissance scholar, a stimulating lecturer, a prolific writer, a perceptive critic of Western civilization, and a leading author of children's novels.

But C. S. Lewis was a Christian, and it is his writing, lecturing, and preaching on behalf of his faith that brought him the greatest fame. His prominent role as a lay theologian in the mid-twentieth century paralleled that of G. K. Chesterton in the earlier twentieth century. Lewis had a dazzling literary versatility, ranging from the monumental study in literary history, *English Literature in the Sixteenth Century Excluding*

Drama, to seven children's novels, from a scholarly study of allegory in medieval times to a trilogy of science fiction novels, from gripping devotional meditations to sparkling religious satire. Many of his more than thirty books deal either directly or indirectly with the Christian faith. Virtually all his books are in current editions and have been published in paperback editions. His Christian writings have been religious best sellers and have been translated into many languages. His pervasive influence in modern Christianity is widely recognized.

A Christian writer who achieves popular acclaim almost inevitably becomes controversial. C. S. Lewis is no exception. He gained both powerful admirers and powerful antagonists. He was showered with undiluted praise and carping criticism both without and within the church. If a man is measured by the enemies he has made, Lewis has attained unquestioned eminence. He has been attacked by theologians, by Christian liberals and Christian fundamentalists, by a wide assortment of unitarians, rationalists, atheists, agnostics, positivists, humanists, and pragmatists. Lewis' uncompromising orthodoxy, his opposition to certain contemporary forces and ideas, his disarming use of satire and irony, his "take it or leave it" attitude toward the Christian faith, alike combined to form an army of heterogeneous critics. Lewis was no bland, pallid, neutral figure; he often produced volatile reactions, both positively and negatively.

Frequently the evaluations of Lewis are emotional and uncritical. R. C. Churchill, a theological liberal, charges that Lewis "is simply using the Church as an excuse for his dreary attacks on everything he hasn't bothered to understand," [1] and that his radio talks "have done a grave disservice to European civilization, of which Christianity at its finest has formed a very important part." [2] Margaret Masterman bristles at his satire and notes that as a schoolboy Lewis was always being told: "'Now then, Lewis, take that look off your face.' Now he needs to be told, 'Wipe that taunt off your pen.'" [3] On the other hand, one of his most ardent admirers, Clyde S. Kilby, feels "that Lewis's apocalyptic vision is perhaps more real than that of anyone since St. John on Patmos." [4] Obviously, he has neither undermined European civilization nor achieved the apocalyptic pinnacle of John.

Whatever the estimate of his achievement, his success as an author gained a vast audience for the hearing of the Christian faith. Few modern Christian writers have been more commercially successful. The irony is that this respected literary scholar, a layman with no formal training in theology, has become the foremost, if not the most influential, of modern apologists for the Christian faith.

That eminence is recognized by a wide variety of critics, friend and foe alike. One of his most severe Christian critics, W. Norman Pittenger, himself a liberal apologist, considers Lewis the "best known and most admired" of popular apologists. While admitting that "it seems to be a fashion nowadays to quote Mr. Lewis as if he were one of the church fathers, along with Augustine and Chrysostom and Athanasius," he warns that Lewis "is a dangerous apologist and an inept theologian." [5] Alistair Cooke, writing in *The New Republic*, fears "that the personal values of several million Britons and Americans stand in imminent danger of befuddlement at which Mr. Lewis is so transparently adroit." [6] Both critics testify to Lewis' popularity and influence.

One fact is beyond dispute: C. S. Lewis was a believing Christian who could write and was read by men. He has spoken to millions of people in his radio talks and through his books, if sales are any indication. Lewis did have an impact on people. He was the most popular lecturer at Oxford and Cambridge for many years. His coming to Cambridge sparked what one of his critics called an "obscurantist recession." Tom Driberg, writing in *The New Statesman and Nation* in 1955, called Lewis "the most popular theologian of the day," and appraised his effect on the university by noting that "nobody at Cambridge seems to have heard of original sin until quite lately." [7] According to this critic, Lewis was apparently having more theological influence at Cambridge than the theological faculty.

Popularity itself is a mark against Lewis for some theologians. Gourmets denigrate plain food eaten by the masses; theological esoterics may be scornful about theology consumed by the masses. Lewis has been accused of patness, of glib oversimplification, and of obliviousness to the finer points of difficult questions. But the fact remains that he has been heard, and through him the Christian gospel has been heard.

That raises an important question. Why should this lay theologian receive such a wide hearing when more highly trained and theologically competent theologians have engaged in dialogue only within a theological isolation booth? What is there about his faith, his view of the world, and his apologetic method that strikes a responsive chord in the hearts of unchurched people?

Lewis, as an apologist, did not fit the common mold. He was called an "apostle to the skeptics" and an "unorthodox champion of orthodoxy." And he was, to say the least, unorthodox in his apologetic method. Several of his books would be classed as traditional apologetics but most have the stamp of the unusual — the infernal correspondence of Screwtape, the haunting myths of the space trilogy, the allegory of the Narnia books — as they all bring the reader face to face with transcendental values and existential questions. Can these writings, despite most of them not being "classic" apologies, legitimately be called "apologies"?

More fundamentally, this raises the question of the nature and function of apologetics. Does apologetics consist of academics talking to academics; of arid, abstruse, systematic rehashing of perennial problems within a limited, esoteric, theological eddy? Or should the apologist wade into the mainstream of life, confronting modern problems and encountering the masses of men, gaining a hearing for the Christian faith by any possible method? Is there a place for living and vital, imaginative and poetic, Christian apologies, which are aimed not at academics but at men in the street who worship the gods of the marketplace?

Lewis, by his own admission, was not a trained theologian. But for that very reason he may have some vital lessons to contribute to ivory-tower apologists and theologians who dialogue with their own kind, have an aversion to being old hat or out of step with the contemporary scene, and who can be both isolated and insulated from the common masses who share neither their capacity for nor their interest in the finer points of theology. Lewis was, after all, a remarkable man who was equally famed as a literary scholar and as a Christian apologist. He mastered the art of communication, and, perhaps, had some insight into what should be communicated. As one of the best-read men of his age, Lewis can offer more specialized apologists refreshing and valuable insight into some of the knottiest problems of modern apologetics. We do not have to be blind to his theological shortcomings, but we cannot afford the luxury of *ipso facto* disregarding Lewis simply because he was " popular." There is a value for theologians in examining Lewis, as a layman who stands outside theological circles, and his writings to see his view of the modern world, his appraisal of theological discussions in the modern church, the foundations of his thought, the theology that he finds basic and relevant to the needs of modern man, and the literary devices and techniques he used to present that theology to the world.

Certain limitations to this apologetic study should be stated. It is not our purpose to estimate Lewis' literary contribution or grade him as a writer. That must be left to those with more expertise in literature. Nor is it our intention to pigeonhole him theologically and attach an "ism" to his views, a danger against which he himself warns us. It is our intention not to make a value judgment on his theological position — other than to indicate certain clarifying insights he contributes and some obvious weaknesses — but to elucidate his thought. We shall attempt also to avoid what Lewis suggests is a frequent tendency of critics — to read into the author what we want, as has been done to Lewis, but rather to make him say neither more nor less nor other than what he says. Nor do we propose to attempt source-hunting, except to indicate the main influences on his thought. We shall further attempt to avoid lapsing into what Lewis calls "the personal heresy" of explaining his work as a manifestation of his psychological needs, except to indicate where the main elements of his own spiritual and intellectual pilgrimage have become the main elements in his apologetic writings.

Our interest is in the influence of Lewis as an apologist and in what others of us may usefully learn from him about how to present the Christian gospel to the contemporary world. As much as possible, we shall try to avoid projecting any personal theological viewpoint on, or because of a personal theological viewpoint reacting from, Lewis. Rather, we shall try to stand in his shoes and see the world and the Christian faith through his eyes. This procedure alone can prevent an initial "critical" excess of enthusiasm or negative reaction and allow us to hear carefully what C. S. Lewis says. Only then, as he suggests as a principle of literary criticism, will we be in a position to make an evaluative judgment of his apologetic method.

The Nature and Purpose of Apologetics

Surprisingly, contemporary apologists do not agree on what Christian apologetics is all about. There is broad disagreement as to the definition, function, method, and purpose of apologetics. Several unresolved questions emerge. Can a distinction be made between "apology" and "apologetics"? Is apologetics a scientific system or an attempt to defend the faith? Is apologetics the act of defending the faith or the study of the ways and means of defending the faith? Is apologetics by Christians for Christians or by Christians for the outside world? Leading authorities can be found advocating different sides of all these questions.[8]

Although scholars disagree about technical questions relating to apologetics, Lewis clearly understood his own role as an apologist. There were three essential facets in his purpose: (1) to present the Christian faith to unbelievers, (2) to defend the Christian faith on behalf of his uneducated fellow Christians, and (3) to defend traditional Christianity. In the Preface to *Mere Christianity*, Lewis states: "Ever since I became a Christian I have thought that the best, perhaps the only, service I could do for my unbelieving neighbours was to explain and defend the belief that has been common to nearly all Christians at all times." [9]

While his books have helped Christians, particularly those like *Reflections on the Psalms* and *Letters to Malcolm: Chiefly on Prayer* which are written for Christians, in the majority of his Christian writings Lewis has the unbeliever in mind. To a critic who charged that he had substituted "smart superficiality for careful thought," Lewis replied, "Most of my books are evangelistic." [10] His evangelistic purpose helps explain both the subjects and the level of his writing. For this reason he did not deal with points of high theology or ecclesiastical history that divide the church, both because he felt they were safer in the hands of experts and because the discussion of disputed points does not help to bring unbelievers into the Christian faith. He further believed that more talented authors were engaged in controversial matters "than in defence of what Baxter calls 'mere' Christianity." [11] Because in his judgment our common belief was not being presented effectively to those outside the church, Lewis took up his apologetic pen.

His evangelistic purpose did not mean that he had no concern for defending the faith on behalf of believers. Actually, Lewis felt that Christian intellectuals have an apologetic obligation to their uneducated brethren. In arguing for the value of Christian learning, he wrote that for the Christian "to be ignorant and simple now — not to be able to meet the enemies on their own ground — would be to throw down our weapons, and to betray our uneducated brethren who have, under God, no defence but us against the intellectual attacks of the heathen." [12]

Lewis' third apologetic purpose was to explain and defend what has been held in common by nearly all Christians at all times. He contends that a "standard of plain, central Christianity" can be found in a wide variety of great Christian writers in all ages, ranging from Puritan Bunyan through Anglican Hooker, Thomist Dante, Spenser and Walton, Pascal and Johnson, Law and Butler, the Elizabethans, to Milton. Before becoming a Christian, Lewis had encountered an "unvarying something" — which he calls "mere Christianity" — in all these writers and in many more. "It was, of course, varied; and yet — after all — so unmistakably the same." [13] He became a Promulgator of the traditional orthodoxy that he thought cuts across varied Christian communions and the whole Christian era. His remarks about *The Problem of Pain* are applicable to all his apologetic writings: "If any parts of the book are 'original,' in the sense of being novel or unorthodox, they are so against my will and as a result of my ignorance. I write, of course, as a layman of the Church of England: but I have tried to assume nothing that is not professed by all baptised and communicating Christians." [14]

As an apologist, Lewis does not do certain things in his writings. He creates no comprehensive, all-embracing apologetic system, and yet he deals with a surprising number of apologetic problems. Sprinkled through his writings are approaches to the problems of revelation, miracle, pain, the relationship of faith and reason, the existence of God, the authority of the Bible, hermeneutics, language, science, philosophy, history, prayer, providence, and ethics. His treatment of these problems, however, is neither systematic nor scientific in the sense of gathering evidence and amassing arguments in support of the Christian faith. Nor does he thoroughly, systematically, and exhaustively deal with objections to the Christian faith. Instead, he generally isolates and deals only with the main problems of a given question.

Further, Lewis does not spend time studying the ways and means of defending the faith; he simply begins to defend and preach the faith. He demonstrates instead of teaching his own ways and means of defense. Lewis is consciously not an innovator, either in theology or apologetic method. He creates no new apologetic method in the sense of having an integrating theme and a unique theological approach. Consequently, he offers no comparison to Søren Kierkegaard's existentialism, Paul Tillich's "method of correlation," or Rudolf Bultmann's "demythologizing."

And yet, it is his method, understood as a way of making apologetic, that sets him off from many other modern apologists. His method, which is inseparable from its literary vehicles, is dictated by his own peculiar literary talents that imprint his works with grace, style, biting wit, and creative imagination. His great literary versatility permits him to utilize numerous apologetic forms, ranging from imaginative novels to poetry, from allegory and myth to discursive reasoning, from formal lectures to preaching, from symbolic children's novels to popular radio talks, from moving, devotional meditations to disarming satire. He is like the fisherman who uses many rods with a variety of bait, bait appealing to quite different fish, but with each having the identical purpose of catching fish. So one person may first meet Lewis in the children's novels, another in the space novels, another in Screwtape, another by hearing his sermons, and be drawn farther into his works until he is confronted with Lewis' "mere" Christianity.

C. S. Lewis: The Man and the Author

The popularity of Lewis as an apologist stems from more than his considerable literary talent. His position of eminence in the world of scholarship, his status as a lay theologian, his commitment to Christian orthodoxy, and the widespread knowledge of his spiritual pilgrimage all contributed to his impact. More important, C. S. Lewis was an atheist who became a Christian. He traveled a circuitous path to God, and his own moral, spiritual, and intellectual experience colors and illuminates his later writings, giving him perceptive firsthand insight into many problems confronting the Christian apologist. Lewis came from a home with the outward trappings of religion — church attendance and a prayer book — but devoid of any vital religious experience. As a young schoolboy, Lewis affirmed the Christian faith; but occultism, religious relativism, the problem of pain, and an ingrained pessimism led him to atheism, which was accompanied by a loss of virtue, at the age of fourteen.

From this point on, Lewis was torn between a longing for what he calls "Joy" and scientific materialism. This *Sehnsucht*, or desire for Joy, became the goad that would ultimately drive Lewis to God. Philosophically, Lewis moved from "popular realism" to philosophic idealism, then to pantheism on to theism, and finally, to Christianity. Having been committed to these viewpoints, Lewis could appreciate their strengths and expose their weaknesses. He catalogs his spiritual and philosophic pilgrimage in his first Christian writing, the allegorical *The Pilgrim's Regress*. The amoral atheist who becomes a Christian has a seemingly inevitable advantage in gaining access to the minds of people who are in the throes of spiritual decision. In effect he can say, "I drank from the same cup that you drink from, and here is why I found it too bitter to swallow."

Lewis' fascinating spiritual autobiography is contained in his *Surprised by Joy: The Shape of My Early Life* which is the main source for facts about his early days. A withdrawn man, Lewis desired to keep his private life obscured from the glare of publicity, and there is no wealth of detailed information about his life. But two other main sources for biographical data do exist: Chad Walsh's *C. S. Lewis: Apostle to the Skeptics*, which was published in 1949, and Clyde S. Kilby's recently published *The Christian World of C. S. Lewis* (1964). Kilby's book benefits from a lifetime of reading Lewis' books, and of correspondence with him.

THE APOLOGIST

Heredity and environment shared in the formation and helped to determine the destiny of C. S. Lewis. He was born into the home of Albert James and Flora Augusta Hamilton Lewis in Belfast, Ireland, on November 29, 1898. The Hamiltons and Lewises were different in temperament and origin. His father, a solicitor, was a member of the first generation of professionals in a family line of Welsh workers. His paternal grandfather was a self-made man who became a partner in an ironworking firm. His mother, the daughter of a clergyman, came from a family of clergymen, lawyers, and sailors. Lewis' father had a true Welsh temperament, with a high capacity for sentiment, passion, extremes of emotion, a love for rhetoric, a quixotic sense of honor, but without a high degree of happiness. The mother was cheerful and tranquilly affectionate. Both parents were bookish people and acquired a voluminous library.

Many childhood elements conspired to develop the boy into Lewis, the Christian and the author. Good parents, a garden, an unrefined but gay and good peasant nurse, and an older brother influenced his early childhood. The nurse taught them of the peasantry of County Down. The brothers shared an interest in drawing and writing, with C. S. being preoccupied with anthropomorphized beasts in Animal-Land. These early years were a period of humdrum and prosaic happiness. There was an absence of beauty, a rarity of aesthetic experiences, and a total lack of religious experience. They were unimaginative, except for his brother's toy garden and the Castlereagh Hills that they viewed through their nursery window, the unattainable hills which first taught Lewis longing, the first taste of *Sehnsucht* in his experience.

The year 1905, when Lewis was seven, marked a transition in his life. Growing prosperity allowed the father to build a large, new country home. Soon the older brother was sent to boarding school, and C. S. began his home education, his mother teaching him French and Latin and a governess everything else. He lived with his parents, his deaf grandfather Lewis, maids, and a bibulous gardener. In the big house, Lewis was surrounded by spaciousness, solitude, and books. Out of doors was a sweeping vista of wide fields stretching to Belfast Lough, with the Antrim hills in the distance, which created the symbol for longing and desiring that recurs frequently in his later writings. Lewis' manual clumsiness provided the motive, the solitude the opportunity, and an attic "study" the environment for the development of his literary and artistic talents. During these middle childhood years, he read voraciously, and, in his attic study, he wrote and illustrated his first stories. In these days of solitude, Lewis lived in his imagination, writing and illustrating stories, then writing a history, about Animal-Land. The stories had interest, character, and humor but neither poetry nor romance; they were prosaic.

Yet, in this period lie the roots of the *Sehnsucht* that becomes the dominant motif of his spiritual seeking. Three particular experiences fired his imagination and awakened in him the longing for Joy, the experience "of an unsatisfied desire which is itself more desirable than any other satisfaction." [15] The first was prompted by a flowering currant bush that reminded him of his brother's toy garden, provoking a brief, intense desire for some undefined object. The second was the discovery of the idea of autumn in Beatrix Potter's *Squirrel Nutkin*. The third was the encounter with the idea of northernness in epic poetry like *The Saga of King Olaf* and *Tegner's Drapa*. This Joy, or unsatisfied desire, is distinct from happiness or pleasure, sharing with them only "the fact that anyone who has experienced it will want it again." [16] Apart from that, it could almost as well be called a kind of unhappiness or grief.

The death of his mother in 1906, when Lewis was eight years old, had several important results. The uncontrolled emotions, incalculable temper, and unjust actions of his father drove the boys from himself and toward each other. Her death was the occasion of Lewis' first feeble prayer to a magician god to work a miracle in his mother. Security and settled happiness disappeared from his life, though fun, pleasure, and stabs of Joy yet remained.

The year 1908 marked the beginning of Lewis' formal education at a succession of boys' schools. He and his brother were first sent to a private school in Hertfordshire, England. The headmaster was a cruel, half-mad man, who punished more than he taught his few students. Here Lewis learned gregariousness, but his fear of emotion increased because of the headmaster's unpredictable and violent emotional extremes. Here Lewis first became an effective believer in a high " Anglo-Catholic" church, began to pray and read his Bible, and attempted to obey his conscience. A decline in his imaginative life also occurred. The school finally folded in 1910. During this period, the boys were further alienated from their father and were without close friends at home.

In 1910 Lewis was enrolled at Campbell College, a public school near his home in Ireland. Illness forced his withdrawal during his first term. At the age of thirteen, in 1911, he entered a preparatory school called Chartres, which was connected with Wyvern College where his brother was a student. Chartres provided a clever and patient teacher, good food and care, and real friendship. Here Lewis lost his faith, his virtue, and his simplicity. The occultist dabbling of the school's matron excited Lewis but led him into religious relativism. That, coupled with the problem of pain, the problem of comparative religion, and his intellectual pessimism led him into atheism. A new headmaster recently graduated from college taught him about the world, including sophistication, dressiness, "inside" information about the theater, and the latest jokes. Through him simplicity succumbed to vulgarity. At Chartres, Lewis' lust was first awakened by a dancing mistress, and here he succumbed to an assault on his chastity without any guilt or inhibition. For this reason, Lewis has said, "I have been a converted Pagan living among apostate Puritans." [17]

A turning point in Lewis' life occurred at Chartres: he rediscovered Joy — "the stab, the pain, the inconsolable longing." In a literary periodical Lewis' eyes read the title *Siegfried and the Twilight of the Gods*, which was accompanied by an

Arthur Rackham illustration, and pure "northernness" engulfed him, and he knew that to have Joy again was the supreme object of desire. Shortly after, he was enamored with Wagnerian music for the same reason. "Northernness" became more important than anything else and led to an imaginative Renaissance, resulting in a new appreciation for nature and an intense interest in Norse mythology. Lewis' secret, imaginative life became distinct from his outer life, his inner life being concerned only with Joy and his outer life, including much normally called imagination, concerned with everything else.

This division of his life into inner and outer was accentuated during his year in Wyvern College, to which he earned a classical entrance scholarship in the summer of 1913. His life there began in ecstasy and ended in hatred of the school. Lewis rebelled against the public school system: the social climbing represented by the Bloods, the urbane, athletic, school aristocracy; the Tarts, the effeminate younger students who served as catamites to the Bloods; the compulsory games; the constant fagging of the younger students; the enforced pretense of interest in boring matters. The rigor of schedule and the lack of privacy made Lewis tired in body and mind, and caused him to hate Wyvern. The realization that his fellow students did not share his literary and artistic interest made him for the first time an intellectual prig. His outer life at Wyvern had only two blessings: Smewgy, his teacher, who taught him Latin and Greek, of the beauty of poetry, and courtesy of manners; and the library, his sanctuary of privacy and books, where he first encountered Celtic mythology.

Yet, at this period, his inner life was one of ecstasy — a life enlivened by mythology, intoxicated with the physical world, and aching with desire. The relation of the sons to their father further deteriorated, as did the relation between C. S. and his brother. At this time C. S. found his first friend, a neighbor boy named Arthur, who shared his interest in Norse mythology and his desire for Joy.

THE APOLOGIST

The decision to send Lewis to a private tutor, W. T. Kirkpatrick, introduced the happiest years of his life, lasting from 1914–1916. Kirkpatrick was a ruthless dialectician and atheistic rationalist who taught Lewis to think and communicate logically and clearly. With Kirkpatrick, Lewis read the Greek and Latin classics, and learned German, French, and Italian. During the holidays, Lewis shared his time with Arthur, from whom he learned an appreciation for the classic English novels and for the ordinary, simple things of life and nature. During this period, Lewis was confirmed and participated in his first Communion in total disbelief.

There was a divorce between his imaginative and intellectual life. He was now preoccupied with the quest for Joy, which had been reintroduced to him by Norse and Celtic mythology, and he learned in the process that Joy is not a disguise for sexual desire and that it cannot be satisfied by the occult or magic. His intellect, now committed to materialism, was repelled by Christianity and its transcendental Interferer God. His reading of Yeats and Maeterlinck, and his discovery of their interest in magic, spiritualism, and theosophy, raised the possibility for him that there was something beyond the material world which was not connected with Christian theology, making him want " to get the comforts both of a materialist and of a spiritual philosophy without the rigours of either." [18]

The turning point of his life occurred at this juncture. Picking up the Everyman edition of George Macdonald's *Phantastes* in a railroad station bookstall in Leatherhead, he crossed a spiritual frontier. In his reading of the book, the object of his longing, which had eluded him because of its distance and divorce from the real world, drew near and transformed the common things of the real world, without itself being changed. A new quality, which he later understood was holiness, entered his longing. " That night," writes Lewis, " my imagination was, in a certain sense, baptised; the rest of me, not unnaturally, took longer." [19] Finding his master in Macdonald, he began voraciously to read all Macdonald's writings.

Lewis took the scholarship exam and was elected to Oxford in the winter of 1916. With his real object being to enter the University Officer's Training Corps, he began residence at Oxford, along with about eight undergraduates, in the summer term of 1917. Completing the ordinary course of military training, he was commissioned a Second Lieutenant in the Infantry and arrived in the frontline trenches in November, 1917, on his nineteenth birthday. During that winter, he contracted trench fever and spent three weeks of convalescence in a hospital. He was wounded in April, 1918, by an English shell that fell short. While in the service, Lewis began reading Chesterton, in whom he discovered the "charm" of goodness.

Lewis returned to Oxford in January, 1919, having undergone a revolution in his emotional outlook from reading Bergson, who taught him "to relish energy, fertility, and urgency." [20] Back at Oxford, he began to make several lifelong friendships. A. K. Hamilton Jenkins continued Lewis' education in the enjoyment of common things, even ugliness. Owen Barfield became his antiself, the man who shared his interests but disagreed with him about everything. A. C. Harwood, a wholly imperturbable man, shared their conversations and fellowship. The new note in these friendships was that by decent pagan standards these men were "good," and Lewis accepted and attempted to live by their standards.

Lewis adopted an intellectual "new look," in which he abandoned pessimism, self-pity, flirtation with the supernatural, and the delusions of romanticism. Several factors spurred this development. Lewis was disgusted by an old Irish parson who had a ravenous desire for some evidence for personal survival. The experience of being confined for two weeks with a man who was going mad, and who had flirted with theosophy, spiritualism, and psychoanalysis, made him averse to romantic longings or unearthly speculations. Then, the new psychology made him want to distinguish imagination from fancy and fantasy. Bergson led him into a Stoical monism and its affirmation of the necessary existence of the Absolute. The conversion of his friends Harwood and Barfield to anthroposophism shocked Lewis, but from his ensuing disputation with Barfield he learned two things: that his acceptance of the contemporary intellectual climate was uncritical, and that realism was epistemologically bankrupt. So, under Barfield's prodding, Lewis moved to idealism and its belief in the Absolute.

Receiving a first in Greats in the summer of 1922 and finding no philosophy posts open, Lewis entered the English School at Oxford. He immediately made friends with Nevill Coghill, a Christian who lived by what Lewis considered archaic virtues. His reading in English further disturbed his outlook. Langland, Donne, Thomas Browne, and George Herbert all moved him, and they shared a Christian viewpoint. He had found the same spiritual overtones in his earlier literary favorites: Macdonald, Chesterton, Johnson, Spenser, and Milton, and, among the ancients, Plato, Aeschylus, and Vergil. Upon graduating with a first in English with an A.B. degree in 1923, Lewis lectured in philosophy for a year. He was elected a fellow in English language and literature in Magdalen College of Oxford in 1925.

Several factors precipitated the final crisis of his spiritual pilgrimage. The reading of the *Hippolytus* of Euripides reawakened his longing. Alexander's *Space, Time and Deity* helped him to distinguish between his longing and the object of his longing. Linking his new insight into the nature of Joy with his idealism, he began to regard men as appearances of the Absolute in which we have unity and for which we yearn. Finding his watered-down Hegelianism inadequate for teaching philosophy, Lewis was driven back into Berkeleyism and began to call the Absolute, " Spirit." A reading of Chesterton's *Everlasting Man*, with its Christian outline of history, made sense to him. To his dismay, Lewis found he could talk idealism but could not live it. Finally, in the Trinity Term of 1929, Lewis became a theist and knelt and prayed, " the most dejected and reluctant convert in all England." [21]

This was a conversion to mere theism, without any belief in

the future life or in Christianity. Lewis began to attend his parish church on Sundays and his college chapel on weekdays because he felt that he ought " to fly his flag " of belief. A study of comparative religion led him finally to the belief that religion had reached its maturity and found its fulfillment in Christianity. Here the pagan myths had become fact. His conversion to Christianity in 1929 was simple and unemotional, occurring while riding to the zoo at Whipsnade. Lewis writes, " When we set out I did not believe that Jesus Christ is the Son of God, and when we reached the zoo I did." [22] And with his conversion, Joy in and of itself lost importance for Lewis; he now knew that Joy had been only a signpost — a bittersweet pain, a longing, a desiring — which pointed to God.

Beginning in 1939, Lewis met on Tuesday mornings in a pub and on Thursday evenings in his apartment with a group of literary friends called The Inklings. They read and discussed what each was writing at the time, having pervasive influence on each other. The permanent nucleus of the group included Charles Williams, J. R. R. Tolkien, and Owen Barfield, among several others. Until his death in 1945, Williams was Lewis' most admired friend. Of Williams' death, Lewis wrote: " No event has so corroborated my faith in the next world as Williams did simply by dying. When the idea of death and the idea of Williams thus met in my mind, it was the idea of death that was changed." [23]

Lewis' literary production began in 1919 with the publication of *Spirits in Bondage,* a collection of poetry. *Dymer,* a narrative poem, was published in 1926. His first Christian work, the Bunyanesque *The Pilgrim's Regress,* received little notice when first published in 1933. However, *The Allegory of Love: A Study in Medieval Tradition,* his first scholarly work, which studied courtly love in the Middle Ages and the development of the allegorical form, earned him the Hawthornden Prize in 1936. Then came a steady succession of literary works. The first of his space trilogy, *Out of the Silent Planet,* appeared in 1938, followed by *Rehabilitations and Other Essays,* and *The Personal*

Heresy: A Controversy in 1939. His provocative book *The Problem of Pain* was published in 1940.

But Lewis rocketed to fame as a Christian apologist only when *The Screwtape Letters* began to appear serially in *The Guardian*. Compiled into a book in 1941, *Screwtape* immediately became a best seller and made Lewis a world-famous author. The B.B.C. quickly contracted him for a series of broadcasts lasting for a period of three years, talks later compiled as *Broadcast Talks* (1942), *Christian Behaviour* (1943), and *Beyond Personality: The Christian Idea of God* (1944), and published later in the one volume *Mere Christianity* (1952). During the war, Lewis gave lectures on theology at R.A.F. bases. His broadcast talks and R.A.F. lectures made his one of the most familiar voices in Britain.

Lewis had a prolific and versatile literary output. From 1938 until his death in 1963, hardly a year passed without at least one, and sometimes more, of his books coming from the presses. His publications in the 1940's included *A Preface to Paradise Lost, Perelandra, That Hideous Strength, The Great Divorce: A Dream, The Abolition of Man, Miracles: A Preliminary Study,* and *Arthurian Torso*. Beginning in 1950, his Narnia books for children were published, one each year. *The Last Battle* won the Carnegie Medal for the best children's novel in 1956. The mid-1950's saw, in addition to the children's novels, the publication of three quite varied works: the historical study, *English Literature in the Sixteenth Century Excluding Drama*, in the Oxford history of literature series; his autobiography, *Surprised by Joy*; and his mythical novel *Till We Have Faces: A Myth Retold*. Beginning in 1958, his scholarly and Christian writings included *Reflections on the Psalms, The Four Loves, Studies in Words, An Experiment in Criticism,* two books of collected essays and sermons — *The World's Last Night and Other Essays* and *They Asked for a Paper* — and his pseudonymous devotional classic, *A Grief Observed*. Posthumous publications include *Letters to Malcolm: Chiefly on Prayer, The Discarded Image: An Introduction to*

Medieval and Renaissance Literature, and *Poems.*

Aside from his literary fame, Lewis became a stimulating lecturer, and for some years his lectures were the most popular at Oxford and Cambridge. During the war Lewis occasionally preached, usually at Oxford. It was said that only he and Archbishop Temple could fill the University Church to capacity. St. Andrews University in Scotland recognized his theological attainment by awarding him the Honorary Doctor of Divinity in 1946, Lewis being about the only layman so honored there.

Lewis was appointed to the Chair of Medieval and Renaissance Literature at Cambridge in 1955. A lifelong bachelor, Lewis finally in 1957 married Joy Davidman Gresham, a poet and novelist, who had been converted partly through his writings and was then serving as his secretary. She and her former husband, William L. Gresham, had been atheists and communists before becoming Christians. But the Gresham marriage ended in divorce, and she went to England. Shortly before their marriage, it was discovered that she had cancer. Lewis' marriage to Joy Davidman gave him three years of intense marital happiness. After several apparent recuperations had falsely raised their hopes, she died in June, 1960, leaving Lewis as the guardian of her two children. Her death plunged Lewis into grief, the process of which he described in his pseudonymous *A Grief Observed* (1963).

A serious illness in the winter of 1961–1962 forced Lewis to retire temporarily to his house in Headington with his brother. He returned to Cambridge in the fall of 1962 but resigned his chair at the end of that year. He suffered a heart attack and died on November 22, 1963.

II

THE APOLOGETIC SCENE

THE APOLOGIST'S OWN *Sitz im Leben*, the thought patterns and social forces contemporary with him, condition his apologetic approach. How he views the world situation *determines* it. The fact that the content of his apologetic is traditional Christian orthodoxy would lead one to expect Lewis to view the world as essentially unchanged in the past several centuries. Such is not the case.

An accurate analysis of Lewis' attitude toward the modern situation is made difficult by the diversity of his literary genres. His view is often couched in satire or caricature or embedded in myth. He tends to overstate the case in satire and to soar into poetic flight in the myths. But on the basis of his straightforward writings, the satires and myths can be analyzed with some accuracy. When they are, a vivid picture of his world view emerges.

THE WORLD AS IT OUGHT TO BE

Perhaps his appraisal of the contemporary situation can be seen more accurately when contrasted with his view of the world as it ought to be. He has been charged with advocating " medievalism with a vengeance." And it is true that his view of the universe and the destiny of man conflicts with the prevailing outlook of the twentieth century. For Lewis the whole universe is the created realm of God and is alive with his presence. He is present in each created thing but not necessarily in the same mode. The higher the created thing, the more God is present in grace; the lower, the more in power. The motion of the stars and galaxies and all matter in the universe, from the atoms to living organisms, harmonizes in a Great Dance, a *Te Deum*, in praise of God. It is not the dead universe of modern science but is pulsating with life and activity, an aliveness that to the sensitive observer produces numinous awe and wonder. So Lewis can describe Merlin in *That Hideous Strength* as "the last vestige of an older order in which matter and spirit were, from our modern point of view, confused. For him every operation on Nature is a kind of personal contact." [1]

A world crowded with God demands respect and reverence. Much like Buber, Lewis views nature as something with which man should have an I-Thou relationship. It is a world where the lines between animal, plant, and mineral life are minimized. This is what Lewis is saying in the Narnia series where there are talking trees and the stars are gods who can become human. Inanimate nature cannot in his view be analyzed merely into energy. In one of the Narnia stories a boy says, "In our world a star is a huge ball of flaming gas." He is answered, "Even in your world, my son, that is not what a star is but only what it is made of." [2] The same animation of life results in intercourse, courtesy, and respect between the species. In Narnia the lines between the species are minimized: there are humans, beasts, talking beasts, and half human and half animal creatures like the satyrs and fauns. This is what Lewis means in saying that Ransom "had brought back with him from Venus some shadow of man's lost prerogative to ennoble beasts. In his presence Mr. Bultitude [a bear] trembled on the very borders of personality." [3]

What emerges is a hierarchical structure in the universe, from the inanimate world to God himself, in which each created thing finds its unique place within the created order. A principle of masculinity, to which we are all at times feminine, exists within the hierarchy of nature. The principle works out between species, between men and leaders of society, between man and wife, and between man and God. The principle of masculinity requires obedience and humility as erotic, social, and spiritual necessities. In marriage the principle requires that the sexes accept their natural roles: woman, the feminine role of obedience in love; man, the chivalrous combination of manliness and gentleness. God is Absolute Masculinity to whom the whole universe becomes feminine.

Man in "the world as it ought to be" would not be imprisoned incommunicado in the world of sense perception, trapped within the natural order, but would be aware that the natural order is not inclusive of reality. To convince men of the reality of the world beyond nature is the driving motivation of Lewis. He is thinking not of other worlds *within* the universe but of other dimensions of reality, of the Transcendent which is beyond and yet is immanently involved within the created order. This supernatural (or better, sur-natural) world is found in one form or another in virtually all of Lewis' writings. In different analogies and myths, he is saying that the world of nature is only a copy of the real "world beyond nature," and that man's real destiny is not confined to a brief span of years on a fleeting speck of dust in a remote corner of the universe.

Man is made for God, and he lives in a universe where eternal issues are at stake. As a thinking, feeling, desiring, fallen, redeemable creature, man must choose sides in the eternal battle between good and evil. Man "as he ought to be" lives in obedience to God and learns to adjust his soul to reality. All human institutions exist to help man toward that end. Every aspect of life has its proper place within the created order. Consequently, man "as he ought to be" has a healthy acceptance of the world and properly uses all created things — pleasure, food and drink, sex, knowledge, art, work, and social relationships — to the glory of God.

The "world as it ought to be" is shot through with I-Thou relationships — between man and man, man and the animals, man and inanimate nature, and man and God. It is a world overarched by the "world above nature," a world throbbing and pulsating with life. In a moment of nameless terror or delight, man can confront the numinous quality of nature and the mystery of matter and through them find God who is the Source of all longing and desiring and the Destiny of man.

That is the " world as it ought to be "; but what is the " world as it is "? Ransom states the modern situation to Merlin who represents the old: " The poison was brewed in these West lands but it has spat itself everywhere by now. However far you went you would find the machines, the crowded cities, the empty thrones, the false writings, the barren beds: men maddened with false promises and soured with true miseries, worshipping the iron works of their own hands, cut off from Earth their mother and the Father in Heaven. . . . The shadow of one dark wing is over all Tellus." [4]

Our Radical New Era

C. S. Lewis regarded himself as an Old Western Man, as one of the few relics of Old Western Culture yet alive in the twentieth century. That self-evaluation indicates his view of the contemporary situation. The present era is in the midst of the greatest change, not yet complete, in the history of Western man. This was the thesis of Lewis' inaugural lecture (*De Descriptione Temporum*) at Cambridge in 1954. Twentieth-century man, in Lewis' view, is cut off from his historical roots and severed from his past. No previous historical change, however great — whether at the transition from the Fall of Rome to the Dark Ages, the Dark Ages to the Middle Ages, the Middle Ages to the Renaissance, the Renaissance to the Enlightenment — can compare with the change since the time of Jane Austen and Scott (i.e., ca. A.D. 1800).[5]

The Areas of Change

Four areas of life indicate the great change: politics, the arts, religion, and the birth of the machines. Government today, rather than creating order and stability in society, whether in dictatorships or democracies, is by Govertisement, i.e., " government by advertisement," the promotion of mass excitement as the normal organ of political power. Government figures are no longer "rulers" characterized by justice, incorruption, diligence, and clemency; they are "leaders" who have dash, initiative, magnetism, and personality.

Modern art is "shatteringly and bewildering new." Art in no previous age can be compared to the novelty found in the paintings of current Cubists, Dadaists, Surrealists, or of Picasso. Many modern works of art represent neither work nor art, but are only "puddles of spilled sensibility or reflection." Some modern music demands "more talent in the performer than in the composer." Poetry is new almost in a new dimension. Trained readers of earlier poetry found some of it difficult, but they agreed on the answers. In a recent critical symposium on T. S. Eliot's "Cooking Egg," among seven experts, "there is not the slightest agreement among them as to what, in any sense of the word, it means."[6]

The third great change is the "un-christening" of Europe, the emergence of Western culture from the Christian into the post-Christian era. As a cultural change this is more radical than the change from pre-Christian to the Christian era. "Christians and Pagans," thought Lewis, "had much more in common with each other than either has with a post-Christian. The gap between those who worship different gods is not so wide as that between those who worship and those who do not."[7]

The factor, however, that has altered man's place in nature and parallels in significance the changes from the Stone to the Bronze Age and from pastoral to agricultural life is the birth of the machines. Machines have had economic and social consequences, but Lewis is more interested in their psychological effect. Technological progress has created a new archetypal image: that "of old machines being superceded by new and better ones." In the minds of the uneducated the "milestones of life are technical advances" and the attainment of new and better goods. The fact that new machines frequently are better than old machines has caused a significant semantic development. We now call "stagnation" what other ages would have called "permanence," consider "primitive" to be "clumsy" or "inefficient," and think of the "latest" as being "best."

When the new archetypal image derived from technological advance is combined with Darwin's theory of biological evolution and with the myth of universal evolutionism (which is different from and antedates Darwin's theory, its two great expressions being in the pre-Darwinian Keats's "Hyperion" and Wagner's *Ring*), the result is the universal evolutionism or developmentalism in modern thought. Lewis defines universal evolutionism as "the belief that the very formula of universal process is from imperfect to perfect, from small beginnings to great endings, from the rudimentary to the elaborate: the belief which makes people find it natural to think that morality springs from savage taboos, adult sentiment from infantile sexual maladjustments, thought from instinct, mind from matter, organic from inorganic, cosmos from chaos." [8] Lewis considered this to be "the deepest habit of mind in the contemporary world."

Chronological Snobbery

Belief in inevitable development or progress creates what Lewis calls "chronological snobbery," by which he means "the uncritical acceptance of the intellectual climate of our own age and the assumption that whatever has gone out of date is on that account discredited." [9] In assuming that the latest is the best and the earliest is primitive or superstitious, chronological snobbery has isolated us from the past, made us uncritically captive to prevailing ideas in the present era, and led some people to submit to the tyranny of an imaginary future.

Chronological snobbery enslaves man to the present and fairly recent past, to the idols of his own marketplace. Forgetting that our age has its own characteristic illusions and common assumptions, we regard it as a final and permanent platform from which we can objectively view all past ages. The "Spirit of the Age" — whether an idea is modern, fashionable, and progressive — is the criterion for truth or value. Many modern ideas are not developed from critical thinking or historical study, but are absorbed from the prevailing "climate of opinion." Like Master Parrot in *The Pilgrim's Regress*, we learn, under the tutelage of the Spirit of the Age, to parrot the right contemporary answer to any question. An objective look at our own age would reveal, as in any age, that we have seen certain truths and made certain mistakes. But an objective look requires that one stand outside the present. Only the past provides that kind of platform.

But the past is not available to most moderns, for the evolutionary habit of mind also cuts us off from our historical roots. We have lost the great values and ideas common to previous civilizations — values in religion, morality, politics, education, social relations, economics, culture, and thought. For this reason we are living in the midst of the most monumental change in human history. Indeed, Lewis pictures the isolation of man from the past as being one of the chief weapons of the devil. Screwtape tells Wormwood: "It is most important thus to cut every generation off from all others; for where learning makes a free commerce between the ages there is always the danger that the characteristic errors of one may be corrected by the characteristic truths of another." [10]

Lewis thought the devil had used this weapon with romping success. In evaluating how easily modern men are tempted, Screwtape says, "Remember they know no history." The historically ignorant include not only the uneducated but students and many scholars. Students are cut off from the past by the modern tendency to read only new books about ancient books and ideas. Since the new books share our basic modern assumptions, the student views the past through twentieth-century spectacles.

Even many scholars are prevented from learning from history by what Lewis calls "The Historical Point of View." The historical point of view is not concerned with the truth of a statement, but is diverted into studying the influences on the author, the consistency of the statement with the author's total thought, what phase in the writer's development it illustrates, its effect on later thought, and the history of criticism on the question. Spellbound by chronological snobbery, many scholars allow unexamined, contemporary presuppositions to dictate their evaluation of past history. They tend to extract selectively from a given period the ideas of a great man that transcend his age. Of course, ideas that transcend his age are those which agree with ours. So we find in history only what we want. Thanks to the historical point of view, says Screwtape, " Great scholars are now as little nourished by the past as the most ignorant mechanic who holds that ' history is bunk.' " [11]

Chronological snobbery often results in ignorance and false assumptions about past history, e.g., that the ancients knew nothing about the laws of nature or the immensity of the universe, when they knew both. Unfortunately, many fallacious views go unchallenged because of the dearth of careful historical study, thereby complicating the task of apologetics. An example of our modern " knowing without studying " is in *The Pilgrim's Regress* where Mr. Enlightenment explains to John that his ancestors believed in God because they had not had the benefits of scientific training. Mr. Enlightenment begins John's training by saying:

> " Now, I dare say it would be news to you to hear that the earth was round — round as an orange, my lad."
> " Well, I don't know that it would," said John, feeling a little disappointed. " My father always said it was round."
> " No, no, my dear boy," said Mr. Enlightenment, " you must have misunderstood him. It is well known that everyone in Puritania thinks the earth flat. It is not likely that I should be mistaken on such a point. Indeed, it is out of the question." [12]

The final disastrous result of chronological snobbery is that if we, because of historical ignorance, assume with the character in *The Great Divorce* that " the nightmare fantasies of our ancestors are being swept away," then we must assume that "the best is yet to be" and cooperate with the wave of the future. Forgetting that the future is very largely determined by our present choices, we can be tyrannized and dehumanized by an imaginary future that in turn can wrongly be allowed to determine our present choices. Traditional values can in good conscience be debunked and sacrificed for the sake of some imaginary future good.

Lewis dramatizes the ultimate absurdity in the person of Weston, the scientist in *Out of the Silent Planet*, who justifies his diabolical activity on the basis of the higher good of propogating the human race.

> "Well," said Ransom, . . . "you think you are justified in doing anything — absolutely anything — here and now, on the off chance that some creatures or other descended from man as we know him may crawl about a few centuries longer in some part of the universe."
> "Yes — anything whatever," returned the scientist sternly, "and all educated opinion — for I do not call classics and history and such trash education — is entirely on my side." [18]

Twentieth-Century Naturalism

At the root of our modern evolutionary thought is a philosophical outlook as old as mankind — monism. Different types of monistic thought — such as naturalism, pantheism, realism, empiricism — share in common the belief that all particular things and events are interlocked within the whole of our spatiotemporal order, beyond which nothing exists. Lewis calls monism "everythingism," because it believes that "everything" or "the whole show" is all that exists.

For the sake of simplification, Lewis reduces monism or "everythingism" to two alternative positions. If one starts with God, he is a pantheist; if with nature, he is a naturalist. But either view has the effect of excluding any reality outside or beyond the totality of the natural process. Either view creates a mind-set against the existence of any supernatural principles or powers beyond the purely natural order. Lewis says, "Everythingism is congenial to our minds because it is the natural philosophy of a totalitarian, mass-producing, conscripted age." [14]

When a naturalistic world view is linked to the empirical method of experimentation, "scientism" results. Based on a naturalistic philosophy, the contemporary science "worshipper" attempts to use the empirical method to explain all life and value from phenomena intrinsic to the natural process, so that no area of life is left untouched. Naturalism pervades the atmosphere of the twentieth century. Science provides the age-old philosophy a potent new means of expression so that it practically affects the lives of us all. Naturalistic empiricism is the driving force behind the movement of the twentieth century that Lewis most fears — the process leading to the abolition of man.

The Abolition of Man

The ultimate danger of forces operative within the present era is that they are leading to "the abolition of man," the title of a series of lectures Lewis presented at the University of Aberdeen in 1943. This is a theme which in variegated forms runs through a number of his works. It is a recurring theme in his space trilogy, with *That Hideous Strength* being a dramatization of his academic statement in *The Abolition of Man*. The theme crops up in the Screwtape series, in his essay collections, and occasionally in the Narnia series. This is the indispensable key to his understanding of the modern world, and the explanation of much of his satire, sarcasm, and frontal attacks on various aspects of contemporary life.

This central fear receives emotional thrust from an almost congenital characteristic of Lewis: his distrust of authority and rebellion against collectivism; and his passionate attachment to individualism, to the freedom to think and choose and live, to a man's being his own man. His antipathy to social conformity and his appraisal of many aspects of contemporary life are at root a reaction to the incipient influence of the ultimate threat — the abolition of man. To be a man is to be a rational, feeling, thinking, choosing individual, to adjust the soul to reality, and to resist all forces that manipulate and dehumanize man. This is the golden thread that gives an inner consistency to Lewis' attitude toward such aspects of culture as science, education, psychology, philosophy, government, the arts, and even society. The abolition of man is an ultimate threat toward which we are taking giant strides in the present era.

The abolition of man has been made possible by a process that began early in human history and has been accentuated in the modern era, a process that has led from the depersonalization of nature to the depersonalization of man and, ultimately, instead of man's conquest of nature, to nature's conquest of man. The process is seen in the history of philosophy. Primitive man existed in a living universe filled with will, intelligence, and gods. Every tree was a nymph; every planet, a god. Man himself was akin to the gods. With the advance of knowledge, this rich and genial universe has been emptied of its gods, then of its colors, smells, sounds, and tastes. These have been transferred from objective to subjective experience and are regarded as no more than man's own sensations, thoughts, images, or emotions. In much the same way, the soul or self or mind of man is now regarded as an illusion. Admittedly, the gods and nymphs would not do as they stood, but in banishing dryads from trees, we have also banished values from the objective realm, God from the universe, and the soul from man — which opens the door to terrifying possibilities in the manipulation of man. Mankind can be cut into some new, fresh shape by the arbitrary will of a few people in a generation that has learned how to do it.

What Lewis means by the abolition of man is nowhere seen more clearly than in the area of morality, ethics, and values. Naturalism and empiricism lead to a subjective or emotive view of ethics that denies objective value. Until modern times all teachers and men believed that the universe possesses objective value, so that objects could validly merit our approval or disapproval, reverence or contempt. This conception — called variously Natural Law, or the First Principles of Practical Reason, or First Platitudes, or Traditional Morality, or the Tao — is found in Platonic, Aristotelian, Stoic, Christian, and Oriental forms. In contrast, emotive ethics holds that all statements containing a predicate of value are statements of nothing more than the emotional state of the speaker, and as such are unimportant.

Two possible courses are open to those who reject traditional morality. Moral innovators may attempt to preserve the concept of virtue by basing morality on supposedly nonobjective grounds — such as the utility of sacrifice for the community or on instinct. But these nonobjective attempts do not escape Natural Law or traditional morality; they are arbitrarily extracted from it without any logical justification. A further practical fallacy of the Innovator is that no justification of virtue will enable a man to be virtuous — a fact recognized by traditional morality. Earlier civilizations taught children the Natural Law just as old birds teach young birds to fly. They recognized that without the aid of trained emotions, what Plato calls man's spirited element, the intellect is powerless against the animal organism. In fact, argues Lewis, by the spirited element — which is the liaison officer between cerebral and visceral man — man is man. To rip out sentiment and trained emotions is to dehumanize man, a course followed by the Innovators. The Innovators produce "men without chests," men whose emotions have not been disciplined by knowing and practicing the objective values of the Natural Law or the Tao. Then the Innovators expect from barren men the virtue they have rendered impossible.

A more honest approach for those who reject traditional morality is to abandon the concept of value altogether and to make man what we want him to be. Having mastered nature, we now master man and choose our destiny. At some future stage, by the use of contraception, eugenics, prenatal conditioning, and a perfectly applied psychology in education and propaganda, man will obtain full control of himself — which will in fact mean the subjection of the masses to a handful of Conditioners, and through them to nature itself. The Planners of that future generation, a few hundreds of men, will become the rulers of billions of men and all future mankind. These Planners or Conditioners, having abandoned the concept of value, and armed with scientific technique and the powers of an omnicompetent state, will determine the values, the destiny, and the biological and psychological characteristics of future mankind. But lacking transcendental values, the Conditioners will be ruled solely by natural or irrational impulses derived from heredity, digestion, the weather, or the chance association of ideas, but not by the objective values of the Tao. The final stage is when the masses are ruled by the Conditioners, but the Conditioners are ruled by nature — that is the abolition of man.

To Lewis this is no theoretical problem related to remote futurity but an urgent and practical problem in the present. The forces that, if unchecked, will lead to the ultimate abolition of man are already at work. Many mild-eyed scientists, popular dramatists, and amateur philosophers, as well as some communists, fascists, and democrats, are engaged in debunking traditional values and inventing ideologies. Beyond these, nearly all men, some knowingly and some unknowingly, are laboring to produce the rule of the Conditioners over the conditioned human material, the world of posthumanity.

The Major Abolitionist: Modern Science

The main outlet for naturalistic empiricism, the driving force behind the movement toward the abolition of man, is modern science, as it finds expression in the natural and practical sciences; in the human sciences, as represented by Freudianism; and in the application of empiricism to philosophy, as in logical positivism.

As a major abolitionist of man, modern science occupies center stage in a number of Lewis' works and receives some of his most scathing criticism, so much so that some critics charge him with being prejudiced against science. From the amount and range of his scientific polemic he would, on the surface at least, appear vulnerable to the charge. Weston, in *Out of the Silent Planet* and *Perelandra*, is a caricature of the scientifically educated person, the scientific idealist who does not want to chop logic. The National Institute of Coordinated Experiments (N.I.C.E.) in *That Hideous Strength* is a disturbing satire on the pretensions of technology and the social sciences. In *The Abolition of Man*, Lewis charges that science is leading to the dehumanization of man. The whole thrust of *Miracles* is the contraversion of the naturalistic presuppositions of modern science. He slashes at false science in various collected essays in *They Asked for a Paper* and *The World's Last Night*. Science plays a prominent role in *The Pilgrim's Regress*.

Natural Science

A major task for the Christian apologist is to confront the threat of modern science. The threat does not come from "pure" science, but from the "popular" view of science that is propagated in works of scientification and in the thought of little scientists and their little scientific followers. Lewis admits the validity of the scientific method of experimentation, particularly within the physical world, as a way of knowing. But it is no more than that: one of the ways of knowing, with its own values and limitations. Pure science must submit to a limitation of application and epistemological claims. In Lewis' judgment, the great scientists and real natural philosophers accept this view. But science has been apotheosized in the twentieth century, and the popular scientific outlook accepts no limitations. Instead of being *a* way of knowing, it becomes *the* way of knowing. The various criticisms of Lewis against a perverse science can be distilled into two: (1) its epistemological arrogance, and (2) its pretensions of unlimited applicability. Lewis is intent, like Whitehead, Collingwood, and other natural philosophers, on helping to arrest the false course and pretensions of modern science that so affect the outlook and destiny of mankind.

Epistemologically, science depends upon a naturalistic philosophic presupposition that is linked with empiricism as the tool of verification. The method of naturalistic empiricism requires that we reduce nature to analyzable and manipulative quantities, suspend value judgments about it, and ignore its final cause. The fact is that this kind of ruthless analysis and abstraction leaves only an artificial object that is robbed of quality. Whitehead calls this process of abstraction " the fallacy of misplaced concreteness " or " the bifurcation of nature." Whitehead argues that the scientist should exercise " humility before the fact." Lewis says the same thing by indicating that the real scientist will often bow before the mystery of matter and think of realities that he cannot touch or see. But this is not so with false science. Based upon faith in empiricism, it explains away instead of explaining, and forgets that the sum of the parts does not explain the whole and that the abstracted facts of science are not identical with reality. The practical result is the elimination of nonempirical realities, among them objective value, God, and soul.

Far from deriving its naturalistic philosophy empirically from the " facts," science brings its philosophy to the facts. On that basis it constructs the modern scientific world view of naturalistic evolutionary development. And because of science worship, its presuppositions and conclusions frequently go unchallenged. In the popular mind there is " the picture so often painted of Christians huddling together on an ever narrower strip of beach while the incoming tide of 'Science' mounts higher and higher." [15] The whole picture of science professes to be based on inference from observed facts. But the picture in reality is based on the assumptions of the validity of empirical investigation, the validity of inference and human reason, and the uniformity of nature.

The assumptions of science go uncriticized because science has ceased to listen to philosophy and theology. Since the scientific method is regarded as being applicable to any problem, it is no longer interested in accepting other types of human experience. Even so great a biologist as Julian Huxley argues that "any set of phenomena can be treated by the method of science." [16] That kind of epistemological arrogance leads to the unlimited application of science to all areas of life, including philosophy and religion. Modern science was tainted from its birth, Lewis contends, by the impulse to extend man's power to the performance of all possible things. Science shared with its twin brother, magic, the desire to subdue reality to the wishes of men. Increasingly the desire has been extended from physical sciences to the biological, social, psychological, ethical, and now to the religious fields. Lewis was more skeptical of the human sciences than of pure science, believing that the closer science approaches to human affairs the more dehumanizing the effect it has on the scientists. By that rule, chemists and mathematicians would be in less danger than psychologists and sociologists. Lewis has Hingest the chemist in *That Hideous Strength* say: "There are no sciences like Sociology. . . . I happen to believe that you can't study men; you can only get to know them, which is quite a different thing." [17]

The grave dangers that Lewis foresaw from technological and human science are shatteringly dramatized in the characters, institutions, adventures, and conflicts of his space novels: *Out of the Silent Planet*, *Perelandra,* and *That Hideous Strength*. What Lewis most feared is stated by Feverstone in *That Hideous Strength:* "If science is really given a free hand it can now take over the human race and recondition it." [18] Or he again says: "Man has got to take charge of man. That means, remember, that some men have got to take charge of the rest." [19] That is the ultimate threat. As science allows man to subdue all aspects of nature to his own wishes, man in the process is doing things hitherto regarded as disgusting and impious, such as vivisection of animals and men. To Lewis, a regenerate science "would not do even to minerals and vegetables what modern science threatens to do to man himself." [20]

Lewis' opposition to the wrong kind of applied science is seen in his attitude toward such apparently unrelated things as vivisection, criminal rehabilitation, eugenics, experimental education, and technology's harnessing the powers of nature. Not surprisingly, the N.I.C.E. in *That Hideous Strength* engages in all these practices, which in common can lead to the dehumanization of man. Naturalists can easily move from vivisection of animals to experimentation on inferior or captive men, as did the Nazis. Manipulation of man can occur in criminal rehabilitation or in experimental education where a few educators, psychologists, and sociologists determine what kind of "treatment" to effect on their subjects. Through eugenics a few men would be able to determine the course of future generations. Lewis' fear of the possibilities when science is applied to man is well summarized when Feverstone sets forth the intentions of the N.I.C.E., which are: "At first — sterilization of the unfit, liquidation of backward races, (we don't want any dead weights), selective breeding. Then real education, including pre-natal education. . . . A real education makes the patient what it wants infallibly: whatever he or his parents try to do about it. Of course, it'll have to be mainly psychological at first. But we'll get on to biochemical conditioning in the end and direct manipulation of the brain." [21]

While the social scientists are beginning to work on man himself, the technologists have long been at work on nature. The Planning Ghost in *The Great Divorce* wants "to dam the river, cut down the trees, kill the animals, build a mountain railway, smooth out the horrible grass and moss and heather with asphalt." [22] An aim of the N.I.C.E. is to eliminate excess animal and vegetable life from the planet. Already our technology has turned inanimate nature into dust bowls and slag heaps. Advanced civilizations have used their scientific resources to exploit, corrupt, cheat, and enslave primitive peoples. The technicians hope to put the good life within the reach of man, but the truth is that they create as many problems as they cure.

And now scientific technology has advanced to where man stands on the fringe of space. To Lewis this is no happy prospect. He long wondered if the vast astronomical distances of space might not be God's quarantine precaution to prevent the spiritual infection and evil of humanity from spreading to other possibly rational species (if they exist) in the universe. Lewis is sure that the greedy space adventurers and ruthless technical experts will commit the same crimes against other rational species that we have committed against savage peoples on earth. He dramatizes this fear in *Out of the Silent Planet*. Through scientific technicians like Weston, human life will be enabled to make the interplanetary leap to escape the death of our sun and the extinction of life, to move from planet to planet wherever the universe is inhabitable. The preservation of life becomes the greatest good, and no system of morality or inhabitants of other planets may be allowed to stand in its way. Lewis advocates that we now resolve to stand firm against exploitation and imperialism in the universe.

Lewis' attitude toward nature, although not patterned after, closely parallels Albert Schweitzer's "reverence for life." He believes that we must respect the sanctity of all creation, matter as well as spirit, inanimate as well as animate nature. So he can express horror when the earth is raped, or the Narnian "talking trees" capriciously cut down, or the "talking beasts" killed. Nature will have its own revenge when man ceases to respect her sanctity. The judgment on the haters of nature and the human race is described in *That Hideous Strength*, when Lewis says: "Their own strength has betrayed them. They have . . . pulled down Deep Heaven on their heads."[28]

Psychology

Freudianism is the best example of the dangers of science when applied to the study of man. Lewis distinguishes between the medical theories and techniques and the philosophy of Freudian psychoanalysis. He respects and values Freud's authority as a specialist on how to cure neurotics but thinks that when he goes on to talk of general philosophy he speaks as an amateur. The bone of contention again is the epistemological arrogance of human science that projects a whole philosophy from limited empirical facts and by dissecting analysis explains away rather than explains. Lewis criticizes the method, certain theories, and the practical effect of Freudian philosophy. His concern is prompted by the popular impact of Freudianism in the arts, in ethics, in social planning, and in religion. In fact, the new Mr. Enlightenment in *The Pilgrim's Regress* is Sigismund Enlightenment, obviously representing Freud, who is one of the masters of the intellectual climate of the age.

Lewis criticizes certain Freudian theories, not because they are necessarily untrue but because they claim too much. Not satisfied with their being a part of the truth, Freud presented them as the whole truth. In particular Lewis attacked the theory of wish-fulfillment, the theory of symbolism, and the theory of the pathological nature of guilt. When applied to art, for example, the theories of wish-fulfillment and symbolism would trace all art to the fantasies and waking wish-fulfillments of the artist, and all artistic symbols to latent erotic thought. Lewis admits that some art or ideas or religion involve wish-fulfillment and erotic symbolism. What he objects to is the limitation of art, ideas, or religion to these causes; the claim that a work of art, an artistic symbol, or belief in God is " merely " or " that it *all* comes from " wish-fulfillment or erotic disguise. The error is in the " merely," or " nothing more," of the theories. Some modern psychologists make the same claim for all guilt as being " merely " pathological. It is not that some guilt cannot be pathological but that some guilt, far from being pathological, is a normal reaction to moral mistakes. The result of these Freudian theories is that art, traditional beliefs, moral attitudes, intellectual ideas, and religious beliefs are viewed as the products of irrational causes, which is fatal to many human values. Guilt becomes a pathological disorder, value a rationalization of desire, and God a projection of the father image.

When psychoanalysis moves from medical practice to philosophical statement, it must be subject to the rules of logic and reason. But some of the key ideas of Freudianism cannot pass the bar of reason. The theory of symbolism, for example, which may contain truth, argues in a circle. The theory of wish-fulfillment begs the question, and the logical alternatives of the theory cancel each other out. The theory of the pathological nature of all guilt commits the converse fallacy of accident, assuming that what is true under certain circumstances is true in all circumstances. So psychoanalysis wants to use and doesn't want to use reason. The fatal epistemological flaw of Freudianism is its illusion of omniscience.

The psychoanalytic method best illustrates Lewis' reason for resisting the analytical abstraction of science. When psychoanalysis dissects, it doesn't touch the real man. Lewis paints a horrifying picture in *The Pilgrim's Regress* of the Freudian giant making everything transparent by his gaze, so that the innards — the veins, lungs, intestines, brains, larynxes — (representing humanity as bundles of complexes) of all the prisoners in the Freudian dungeon became visible and were presented as the "facts" of existence. Accounts of the unconscious do contain truth that is useful to the physician, but the truth is mixed up with misconceptions. Reason tells John that exposed innards are not the real man; Freudianism only shows what the unconscious would look like if it were exposed. John asks Reason, "But if I cut a man open I should see them in him." And Reason replies, "A man cut open is, so far, not a man." [24]

In Lewis' view, psychology has rightly understood that consciousness is only the film on the surface of the deep. "Their real error lies in underestimating the depth and variety of its contents." There is lightness as well as darkness. "And depths of time too. All my past; my ancestral past; perhaps my prehuman past." [25]

Naturalistic empirical science must not be allowed to arrogate the right from limited empirical facts to project a whole philosophy about the nature of man and reality. Popular psychology, based on Freud, holds many twentieth-century people in its grip. For some it is a grip of death. Lewis laments that those who have been Freudianized too long are incurable.

Philosophy

Lewis valued philosophy and reason but opposed the antimetaphysical trend in modern philosophy. Philosophy was one of the paths that converged into the road back to God for Lewis. Intellectually he moved from popular realism to idealism to pantheism to theism to Christianity, a path allegorized in *The Pilgrim's Regress*. Idealism was a prominent force in the early 1930's, but with its fall a profound change occurred in philosophical thought. A trend that began with the birth of science has been accelerated. Gripped in the throes of naturalism, we have become metaphysically and theologically uneducated. The scientific habit of specialized or truncated thought has increasingly prevented philosophy from getting all the facts necessary for a complete philosophy.

His evaluation of the course of modern philosophy is seen in his view that reason must steer the middle course between cerebral and visceral man, represented in *The Pilgrim's Regress* by the North and South, which are opposite and equal evils. The Northern cerebral men are barren, dry, emotionless men of rigid systems, whether skeptical or dogmatic, and highly organized parties. The Southern visceral men are open to every feeling, attracted by the forbidden and unknown, and willing to cross all frontiers. The Southerners include a diversified group, as indicated by names selected from the Mappa Mundi in *The Pilgrim's Regress*: Wisdom, Aphroditopolis, Thrill, Antinomia, Theosophica, Orgiasticus, Occultica, Hegeliana, Aesthetica, and Anthroposophia. The Northerners include Sensible, the Pale Men (Neo-Anglican, Neo-Classical, and Neo-Humanist), Ignorantia, Zeitgeistheim, Dialectica, and others. Lewis considered our own age to be predominantly Northern — captivated by naturalistic rationalism and fortified against emotion. The problem today is not excess but barrenness of emotion. So Lewis contends that the pressing need in modern education "is not to cut down jungles but to irrigate deserts."[26]

Under the influence of science, the course of philosophy since the 1930's, apart from dialetical materialism, has gone in two main directions: logical positivism and existentialism, representing respectively the North and South. Lewis said little about existentialism, though he admitted he found the existentialists difficult to understand and that his knowledge of the movement was limited. He feared that existentialism carried to its logical extreme imperils the use of reason.

Logical positivism, which was only in its infancy when Lewis wrote *The Pilgrim's Regress*, represents the jumping-off place for naturalistic rationalism. The misuse of reason and the truncation of thought can be carried no farther. So Lewis describes Wither, who represents the absurd extreme of naturalistic empiricism in *That Hideous Strength:* " He had long ceased to believe in knowledge itself. . . . He had passed from Hegel into Hume, thence through Pragmatism, and thence through Logical Positivism, and at last out into the complete void."[27] Logical positivism is the springboard into nihilism. The method that emptied the universe is now used to empty man. In the emptying process, the items of the objective world were first transferred to subjective experiences, and then consciousness became only a "symbol for certain verifiable facts" about man's behavior. Then it was claimed that the symbol was mistaken for a thing. And now logical positivism contends "that our mistake was a linguistic one. All our previous theologies, metaphysics, and psychologies were a product of bad grammar. . . . And thus we arrived at a result uncommonly like zero. . . . Almost nobody has been making linguistic mistakes about almost nothing."[28]

The restriction of philosophy to linguistic analysis prevents its application to metaphysical questions. What can, when properly used, be one of the paths to ultimate truth and God becomes an obstacle which contends that the question and the quest are philosophically meaningless. Beyond this lies only the vacuum of relativity and nihilism.

The Present Stage of Abolition: Mass Conformity

The present stage of man's abolition is seen in his increasing subjection to forces exterior to himself. The successful work of various Conditioners is apparent in what Lewis judges to be most characteristic of modern society: its sterile homogeneity and mass conformity — moral, social, and political; the loss of individuality and the suppression of individual liberty; the reduction of men to ciphers; a false egalitarianism that eliminates excellence; and the lack of reflection and rebellion. The loss of individuality and mass conformity is the beginning of what will culminate in the complete control of the masses by a minority of masters. The loss of individuality, which is being promoted in most departments of modern life, makes the devil's job much easier. "Every dictator or even demagogue," says Screwtape, " — almost every film-star or crooner — can now draw tens of thousands with him. . . . Catch the bellwether and his whole flock comes after him." [29]

Human abolitionists other than modern science and its handmaids are at work in education, government, economics, modern communications and advertising, and even in society itself.

Education

Lewis' marked antipathy toward modern education was provoked in part by his rather pronounced upper-middle-class prejudices. Having been privately educated, with the exception of a few years at select public schools and his years at Oxford, and having come from an educated family and a childhood of solitude and reading, Lewis opposed much of the modern educational trend. State control of education, in his view, constitutes a basic problem. State-imposed "penal" taxes for education are liquidating the middle class, which can no longer afford private education for their children. Now the student must study subjects selected by a few state planners. The planners determine that education will not be concerned with history, the classics, or language. They aim to produce "adjusted" rather than educated students, adjustment, of course, meaning conformity to the norm of the group.

A further problem is that the state is controlled by a perverted idea of democracy, a false egalitarianism that eliminates genius by providing universal education through the university level, regardless of one's ability. Guided by "parity of esteem," state education abandons incentives and penalties for learning and designs examinations so that all students get good marks. Rather than make dull students feel inferior, it provides vocational and hobby education for those who cannot learn mathematics, science, or languages.

Beyond the inadequate educational content, Lewis was convinced that naturalism currently influences various educational disciplines, even his own field of literary criticism. The result is the subtle conditioning of the student against emotion, beauty, transcendental reality, and objective value.

Collectivism, in Lewis' judgment, is also a controlling factor in modern education. Headmasters, who fear both solitude and friendship, force students to live in a crowd. The universities too now keep the student involved in a crowd — in lectures attended by two or three hundred people, and in intellectual "societies" — so that no time is left for privacy or small groups. "We live, in fact," Lewis suggests, "in a world starved for solitude, silence, and privacy: and therefore starved for meditation and friendship." [30] Lewis felt that if an Augustine, a Vaughn, a Traherne, or a Wordsworth were born today, he would soon be cured.

Augmenting the power of the educational machine is the trend to Charientocracy. Since education is increasingly becoming the means of access to the ruling or managerial class, the Charientocracy, the student must convince the ruling class that he is a specific kind of "cultured" person, cultured in the sense of giving the "right" current responses and answers to intellectual and artistic questions. Thus the individual becomes a helpless plasticine for the modern educator. Robbed of solitude, small-group discussion, time for free reading, and access to history and the classics, and motivated by ambition to enter the ruling class, the student masters the art of producing the kind of orthodox responses and analytic method demanded by his teacher. He becomes clay in the hands of the educational planners. Instead of requiring the student to read and remember what he has read and to cultivate individual tastes, education proposes to teach "appreciation" for the right books, the right art, the right ideas, and the right values. And the "right" responses are determined not by individual teachers but by a "culture-mongers central bureau" that tells teachers what they are to prefer and on what grounds. And the bureau keeps a sharp lookout for deviationists.

The practical effect of "modern" education is seen in Lewis' appraisal in *That Hideous Strength* of the brilliant sociologist Mark Studdock's education: "In Mark's mind hardly one rag of noble thought, either Christian or Pagan, had a secure lodging. His education had been neither scientific nor classical — merely 'Modern.' The severities both of abstraction and of high human tradition had passed him by: . . . He was a man of straw, a glib examinee in subjects that require no exact knowledge." [31] Education is a powerful force in the movement toward the abolition of man.

Government, Economics, and News Media

Government. Lewis' distrust of authority is reflected in his attitude toward public life and government. He feared the development of an omnicompetent state, particularly the power potential in the wedding of applied science, sociological planning, and government bureaucracy. He considered this to be a danger in communism, fascism, and democracy. He caricatures this fear in the National Institute of Coordinated Experiments (N.I.C.E.) in *That Hideous Strength*, which he describes as "the first-fruits of that constructive fusion between the state and the laboratory on which so many thoughtful people base their hopes of a better world." [32]

Already the state is curtailing personal freedom. In the democracies the regimentation is produced by a false idea of democracy, that in the name of equality all superiority or individuality is to be suppressed and everyone is to be reduced to the same level, which leads to a nation without great men. Tyranny does the same thing without the ideal of democracy. Lewis believed democracy to be the best form of government, not because men are so good they should share in government but because fallen men are so wicked " that not one of them can be trusted with any irresponsible power over his fellows." [33] Equality is not a part of the natural order, but is a result of the Fall, purely a protective measure against one another's cruelty. For this reason Lewis feared the trend toward the omnicompetent state that is a characteristic of the twentieth century.

Economics. The modern economic situation in fully industrialized societies also victimizes man. A buying-selling economy alters the historic role of work. Products now are manufactured not necessarily because people need them but in order that people may earn money for making them. The result is built-in obsolescence, useless work, creation by advertisement of mass markets for useless products, an international competitive search for customers, and government spending to keep money circulating and factories working.

Work that has the sole purpose of earning money has a debilitating effect on man. It creates an infection in the spirit, an infection clearly seen, thinks Lewis, in some modern artists. Many of them now never think of their duty to humanity, in terms of recognizing our tastes, interests, or habits, but only of humanity's duty to give the artist recognition, appreciation, and support. In other occupations there is a tendency to regard a trade as existing mainly for those who practice it.

The economic involvement of government and the "employment" dilemma of our money economy open serious possibilities for the domination of man. When Feverstone, in *That Hideous Strength*, raises questions about the purpose of the N.I.C.E., Busby justifies it by saying: " It's the first attempt to take applied science seriously from the national point of view. . . . The buildings alone, the apparatus alone — ! Think what it has already done for industry. Think how it is going to mobilise all the talent of the country; and not only scientific talent in the narrower sense." [84] That 1946 prediction of Lewis has already come true in the defense and aerospace involvements of governments in the 1960's, where economic stability is dependent on government spending and subject to governmental control.

News Media. Newspapers and advertising are powerful instruments in the manipulation of man. Modern men have an inability to disbelieve advertisements. Out of automatic response to sexy or snobbish appeals that have the sole purpose of creating a demand or market for the advertised product, they buy useless, ugly, or pernicious luxuries. Lewis was also critical of newspapers, which he felt frequently resort to vulgarity and sensationalism. More importantly, they can control the thinking of their readers, especially the educated readers who are conditioned to believe anything they read in " high-brow " newspapers and magazines. They can become coercive tools of propaganda.

Society

In addition to forces within society — such as education, government, the economy, and communications media — society itself is contributing to the abolishment of individuality and the establishment of conformity. Society is at work on two levels: among the masses, and in the small coteries of individuals that Lewis calls the " inner ring." Mass conformity is fostered by modern society's unacknowledged creed of togetherness or " being like folks " and by the perversion of the political ideal of democracy into a false creed of social equality. Great value is placed on what is modern, fashionable, or conventional. The man who by talent, taste, or preference disregards prevailing standards is regarded as a snob, a prig, or as abnormal. Lewis even indicates that there are no longer any great sinners because men have become so passively responsive to their social environment that there no longer remains the clarity and deliberateness essential to mortal sin.

No one wants to deviate from the prevailing norm. In an age of promiscuity, chastity is unfashionable. Lewis believed that many a virginity has been lost less in obedience to the urge of Venus than in fear of not being a normal twentieth-century person. Probably many persons first smoked or got drunk for the same reason. So honesty, chastity, temperance, or taste for good literature or music are often lost because they might make one different or offend against the modern way of life.

In a post-Christian era, social conformity creates several problems for the Christian apologist. If the Christian faith is out of fashion, the masses hate to deviate from the norm and become Christians. Our current false egalitarianism produces a further difficult problem. In trying to eliminate all excellence or nonconformity, egalitarianism creates an "I'm as good as you" attitude that excludes the humility and charity so essential to finding God. And those who resist conformity increasingly tend to become prigs and cranks who have a sinister pride in being a deviationist, an attitude equally fatal to finding God.

The social nonconformist illustrates another force within society that suppresses individuality and corrupts man: the inner ring. The lure of the inner ring is not unique to the twentieth century but is a perennial problem, one of the dominant elements of life from the cradle to the grave. Its effect is so great that it cannot be ignored by an apologist. Lewis has an address entitled "The Inner Ring," [35] and the idea repeatedly recurs in his writings. The inner ring, which could be called "the group," "the set," or "that gang," is an elite little group which excludes outsiders. It can exist in many forms — at school, among artists, in the professions, in the trades, in politics, in "high society," in any one of hundreds of places.

The existence of groups is unavoidable and not in itself a bad thing. The longing to enter any group whose acceptance one desires, the anguish at exclusion, and the pleasure of getting in is the morally dangerous element. The desire that draws men into the inner rings — the lust for the esoteric, the hunger for the delicious sweet sense of intimacy, the feeling of being bound together against the outside world — can morally compromise the individual. Afraid of appearing crude, naïve, or priggish, the new insider can easily break the rules of fair play or honesty or morality for reasons that outsiders could never understand. The moral pressure of the inner ring is seen in Lewis' description of Mark Studdock's decision to manufacture news. " But the moment of his consent almost escaped his notice; certainly, there was no struggle, no sense of turning a corner . . . for him, it all slipped past in a chatter of laughter, of that intimate laughter between fellow professionals, which of all earthly powers is the strongest to make men do very bad things before they are yet, individually, very bad men." [86] The same chatter of laughter, knowing wink, or thrill from the use of the collective " we " can chain the individual to the standards, tastes, and values of the esoteric group. Fear of being thrust back outside prevents him from ever deviating from the norm.

Lewis has touched on a serious and overlooked practical difficulty for the contemporary apologist: the social forces and institutions that are molding individuals, the ominous power of society to enforce conformity, and the individual's esoteric lust to be accepted by the inner rings. The homogenizing power is at work in society: in those who are afraid to deviate from conventional mores, in the socially insecure student who wants to be accepted in the fraternity or in the university philosophy club, in the man who wants the sweet acceptance of the trade union council or the circle of company management. In-group conformity binds even the professional nonconformist, for example, the " artistically sensitive " *avant-garde* who sit in an espresso cellar for eight hours looking at a one-shot nonmoving motion picture of the spire of the Empire State Building — all with the same style of dress, taste, mores, and even smell. The power is at work wherever men fear to be labeled " deviationists," or where men desire to be in, and are in terror of being left outside of, their particular inner ring. The group shapes and molds the individual. His individual tastes and standards are destroyed. He does what is " in " — whether it is discotheque, watching the eight-hour still " motion " picture, admiring paint reproductions of a soup can, or breaking moral or legal rules because he is an insider to whom they do not apply.

So an individual may have a hunger for God, an inclination toward the Christian faith, and yet be hamstrung by the lure of the inner ring and the homogenizing pressure of society. No apologist will get through who cannot break the stranglehold of society and cause his reader to assert his individuality so that he may truly hear and choose.

The Post-Christian Era

The twentieth century is the post-Christian era in culture and in the temper of men's minds. Europe has been unchristened, not by relapsing into paganism but by moving beyond Christianity. " The post-Christian is cut off from the Christian past and, therefore, doubly from the pagan past." [37] Naturalism has spilled over into the Christian church. Even many clergymen have naturalism in their bones. Instead of confronting naturalism head on, they make every possible concession, so that with the advance of science they are reduced to an ever smaller defensive beachhead on which science has not yet spoken. Naturalistic presuppositions prevent some Christians from accepting the articles of the " faith once given to the saints "; yet they desire that a vestigial religion remain and continue to make converts. So they lighten the load, demythologize, and throw out the supernatural.

Lewis is unalterably opposed to liberal Christianity, which he considers to have sold out the Christian faith. " Liberal Christianity can only supply an ineffectual echo to the massive chorus of agreed and admitted unbelief." [38] It contributes to the forces of secularism in this post-Christian era. From his earliest to his last Christian writings, Lewis assailed liberal clergymen. In *The Screwtape Letters* he portrays the skeptical vicar and the shocking vicar. The apostate clergyman in *The Great Divorce*, in the guise of intellectual honesty and free inquiry, abandoned the orthodox faith, and in consequence achieved popularity, sales of his books, and a bishopric. In *That Hideous Strength* one encounters Busby, the ex-clergyman, and Straik, the mad parson, both of whom represent the " religion " of naturalism. Mr. Broad in *The Pilgrim's Regress* represents modernizing Christianity that puts more emphasis on the language of the heart than on the lifeless views and barren formulas of mere orthodoxy. All these characters are vivid fictional portrayals of what Lewis calls " Christianity-and-water " — the diluted, synthetic religion of liberal Christianity. Although Lewis' judgment of the motives of the liberals tempered as he matured, he never wavered in condemning their assumptions, their views, and their effect in the modern world. He disagreed with the liberal assumption that the world will abandon all pretense of Christianity before it will accept the supernatural. " By the way," Lewis asks Malcolm, " did you ever meet, or hear of, anyone who was converted from scepticism to a ' liberal ' or ' demythologized ' Christianity? I think that when unbelievers come in at all, they come in a good deal further." [39] Lewis felt that liberalism is betraying the need of the post-Christian era and is surrendering unnecessarily to the Spirit of the Age.

Outside the Christian church, and at times within it, where religion exists, it is usually what Lewis regards as the natural bent of man — pantheism. It is the " popular " religion of the twentieth century, and is congenial to those who love to speak of beauty, truth, and goodness, or of a great pervading spiritual force, or of a generalized pool of spirituality. Pantheism is found today in theosophy and worship of the life force, in worship of racial spirit, and in certain forms of emergent evolution and panpsychism. It is suitable to the modern temperament because " the Pantheist's God does nothing, demands nothing." [40] There is nothing to fear and nothing to obey.

Lewis said little about deism as a dominant force, though in *Letters to Malcolm* he suggests that where deism is a problem, as evidently at Woolwich, one must emphasize the divine presence in created things. It would seem that Lewis underestimated the power of deism, at least in the United States where it is a larger problem than pantheism. And yet, Lewis' point is still valid whether with pantheism or deism. Each gives its adherent the comfort of a religious approach to life, the emotional security of believing that a purposive mind is behind the creation and perfecting of the universe. But in either case the god will not be a Transcendental Interferer, the troublesome God of the Christian faith. That is the modern temper. " All the thrills of religion and none of the cost." [41]

Either submerging God within or removing him from creation is equally fatal to the Christian view of a personal, commanding, judging, redeeming God. Two results follow, which Lewis noted. The first is the almost total absence of a sense of sin in modern man. The early Christian preachers could count on a sense of guilt and proclaim the Christian message of good news. Now hearers must be convinced of the diagnosis of sin before they will welcome the remedy. Even the approach to diagnosis has changed. Older preachers spoke of drunkenness and unchastity. But drunkenness is no longer the same problem, and contraceptives have removed the fear of impregnation and with it the sense of guilt in adultery.

The second result follows from the first. Dullness to sin, stemming from a pantheistic or deistic religion, leads to a lack of awe before God. Modern man's attitude to God is brilliantly stated by Lewis: " 'I'he ancient man approached God (or even the gods) as the accused person approaches his judge. For the modern man the roles are reversed. He is the judge: God is in the dock. He is quite a kindly judge: if God should have a reasonable defence for being the god who permits war, poverty and disease, he is ready to listen to it. The trial may even end in God's acquittal. But the important thing is that man is on the Bench and God is in the Dock." [42] The post-Christian man, like Orual in *Till We Have Faces*, is more ready to present a "case against the gods," *if* they exist, than to hear the case of the gods against man. Merlin, if alive, would indeed find twentieth-century men "cut off from Earth their mother and the Father in Heaven." Naturalism, empiricism, and secularism have done their job.

An Appraisal of Lewis' World View

Lewis may not, as Clyde Kilby insists he is not,[43] be a "calamity howler," but he certainly is a signalman trying to flag down the 20th Century Express. Yet it is unfair simply to call him a "Medieval Moralist" and have done with it. It is true that Lewis attacked many of the mainsprings of progress in the twentieth century. But he is not opposed to progress, only progress in the wrong direction. He did put his finger on some of the danger points of contemporary civilization. But as a master of satire, sarcasm, caricature, and the shock technique, Lewis often overstates his case, paints issues in stark black and white, and warns of danger without extolling values. For example, although he scathes applied science for eradicating excess animal and plant life and for harnessing nature, he does not give it adequate credit for vaccines and miracle drugs, for flood prevention, or for progress in transportation. Perhaps that is inevitable for the satirist, but it might alienate the borderline reader who has a lust for "science" and only a yearning (not yet become real longing) for religion.

However, Lewis' view of the modern world is of value to the apologist quite apart from the question of its accuracy or inaccuracy, its balance or imbalance. He teaches us that the apologetic task involves more than an intellectual confrontation with the secular world and more than a scientific statement of the Christian rationale. He teaches us that intellectual objections are often intimately interwoven with other factors — psychological, social, political, and economic; with a naïve acceptance of a naturalistic world view and its uncritical rejection of supernaturalism, including its God who dabbles in human affairs, its antiquated ideas of the fall of man or original sin, its angels and devils, its primitive view of heaven and hell, its transcendental values and meaning, and its divine judgment over the affairs of men.

It is this very understanding of the complexity of our social and psychological, as well as intellectual and spiritual, setting that contributes to Lewis' unique approach to apologetics. He does not rest content with confronting the intellect. Rather, he probes the motives and characters of his readers and exposes psychological and social factors that contribute to unbelief. In other words, Lewis is aware of the power of original sin to corrupt the intellect and prevent the proper use of reason, and to misdirect man's immortal longings. Thus his penetrating psychological insight is of great importance for the apologist. He tries to create what heredity and environment no longer do — a sense of sin and an awareness of God — by probing analysis of the psychology of human behavior and the ominous pressure of society. This effort roots in Lewis' belief that apologetics is more than precise, coherent, finely shaded, scientific defenses of the Christian faith. Apologetics is inescapably evangelistic.

III

THE FOUNDATION OF APOLOGETICS

THE CHRISTIAN APOLOGIST must face certain decisive problems within his study before he faces the non-Christian world. What he does before he makes an apology determines the content, approach, impact, and value of his apologetic effort. He must decide how he knows, what he knows, and how to communicate what he knows. A breakdown at any point is disastrous for an apologetic attempt.

Epistemology is the starting point for any apologist, followed by the corollary problems of hermeneutics and the authority for faith. Having determined the tools for knowing, the apologist must fill his faith with intellectual content in theology and ethics. Then, having settled how he knows and what he believes, he must master the art of communicating the Christian faith to other people. Thus, before a Christian becomes an effective apologist, he must be a philosopher, a theologian, and a master of communication.

EPISTEMOLOGY: THE PROBLEM OF KNOWLEDGE

Lewis the Epistemologist could best be called " the Reasoning Romantic." His approach to the problem of knowledge gives his apologetic a unique character and puts him out of step with much contemporary theology. Reason and imagination are the indispensable and mutually necessary human faculties for knowing. For Lewis, " reason is the natural organ of truth; but imagination is the organ of meaning." [1] No estimation of

Lewis' epistemology is adequate that does not include both reason and imagination in their respective functions.

The epistemological function of reason and imagination for Lewis is rooted in his own experience. Reason and imagination, beginning early in his life and often pulling in opposite directions, were the controlling elements in Lewis' intellectual and spiritual pilgrimage. Imaginative life came natural to Lewis: the *Sehnsucht*, the longing and desire for Joy, fairyland, and Norse and Celtic mythology. Reason was forced on him by his early tutors, so that he demanded evidence for truth and logically consistent thought. He became enamored with ratiocination. In these childhood years, he lived in two worlds. Everything he desired was an object of imagination; everything he believed was an object of reason. After a period of years in which reason and imagination alternated in dominating him, the two faculties began to work in harmony, first one and then the other forging ahead. Reason began to clarify the longing and desire of his imaginative life until his imaginative desire was projected beyond feeling and the transient objects of desire — sex, the occult, and the aesthetic — to the Ultimate Object, God himself. Reason led him through the philosophic "isms" to theism and an intelligent assessment of mature religions. His imagination and reason converged at the point of revelation; and for him revelation pointed to where myth had become fact: the Incarnate God Jesus Christ.

His epistemology grows out of his understanding of the unity of man, that we are neither merely cerebral nor visceral men but thinking and feeling men who by the proper use of these two faculties can be led to God. And both are essential to valid knowledge, reason for logical truth and imagination for meaning. Both involve the individual in dialectic — the imagination in a "dialectic of desire," an ontological or "lived" dialectic; the reason in a dialectic of philosophic argument. So Lewis' "lived" dialectic of imagination and "argued" dialectic of reason converged on one goal.

Both are essential to his epistemology and his apologetic. He uses them in mixed proportions in his writings. Reason is the basic tool in his discursive and didactic writings like *Mere Christianity, Miracles,* and *The Problem of Pain,* although he also tries to awaken the immortal longings of the imagination. Imagination is the basic tool in the myths and allegories, although he also tries to disturb and challenge reason. On the one hand, he uses reason to argue the possibility that Christianity is true. On the other hand, he attempts an imaginative renaissance so that reason, freed from false shackles, may reason correctly.

Lewis' faith in reason sets him against much current theological thought. He could never call reason "a whore" or advocate a Kierkegaardian leap in the dark. Thus he accuses existentialism of "fuzzy thinking." Nor is he compatible with the Barthian brand of neo-orthodoxy which sets revelation over against reason. He is a "ruthless dialectician" who insists that reason not stop short of its ultimate goal: truth. Here lies the error of liberal Christianity: It does not follow reason to its logical end. On the other hand, Lewis' insistence on the function of the imagination brings him into conflict with neo-Thomistic Catholic thought and with the whole demythologizing movement of the present era.

It is difficult to make a *precise* epistemological analysis of the roles and relation of imagination and reason. It is easy to quote a few of Lewis' statements but not to ask what they mean and how they are related. A forty-four-year span of writing and the variety of types of writing by Lewis complicate the attempt. One cannot turn to a specific writing and find Lewis stating his epistemology. He is not even consistent always in the use of terms in different types, or from the first to the last, of his writings. For example, the subtitle of *The Pilgrim's Regress* is "An Allegorical Apology for Christianity, Reason, and Romanticism," in which he gave "romanticism" a purely private meaning. He confesses he later came to see that it has such varying senses as to be useless.

For Lewis, the epistemological function of imagination and

reason can be fully understood only in relation to language. In *The Pilgrim's Regress*, an allegorical spiritual autobiography of Lewis, imagination is intimately bound up with *Sehnsucht*, the longing for ultimate reality which he symbolizes in many ways, and with his understanding of the nature of language and its relation to reality — namely, that ultimate reality can be spoken of only allegorically and mythologically. His *Surprised by Joy* in 1955 treats directly the same experience, and it defines much more precisely the functions of imagination and reason. A development or refinement of his understanding of the role of imagination can be detected between his 1936 study *The Allegory of Love*, and an essay on language, "Bluspels and Flalansferes,"[2] published in 1939, which clarifies his treatment of imagination in *The Allegory of Love* and forms the basis for epistemology in his later writings.

The Origin and History of Language

To understand Lewis' view of the epistemological function of reason, imagination, and language, it is necessary to know his view of the origin and history of language. At this point Lewis acknowledges a debt to his friend Owen Barfield, whose ideas were already Lewis' before Barfield published his *Poetic Diction* (to which one can go for an elaboration of Lewis' view). What follows is a brief attempt to state in understandable terms a difficult, abstruse, and highly complicated but essential idea.[3]

Lewis believes that the origin and history of language reflect a psychophysical parallelism in the universe. There was an ancient unity of human experience quite unlike our modern fragmentation of experience into subject and object, sensible and insensible, intellectual and imaginative, thought and perception, literal and metaphorical. Primitive man did not completely differentiate himself as subject from the world as object, or the phenomenal (sensible) world from the noumenal (insensible) world. Nor did he split *how* he experienced the objective world from *what* he experienced or *how he expressed* what he experienced; there was a unity of the mind that sees, the thing seen, and the language that expresses what is seen. His mental process could be called neither intellectual nor imaginative; rather, his thinking was perceiving and his perceiving was thinking. The overall unity of the knowing process provided primitive man with an immediate qualitative-quantitative apprehension of concrete reality, which is best described as picture-thinking or thought-perception.

Reflecting the primitive psychophysical parallelism in the world and the intellectual-imaginative in the mind, language originally had a unity of meaning that was neither "literal" nor "metaphorical" in the modern sense. Contrary to some modern theories, words did not begin by referring to physical objects, then gradually getting extended metaphorically to emotions, mental states, and general relations. No such dichotomy between physical and spiritual existed. Further, the inseparability of ancient language from thought-perception — which forces one to speak of seeing-saying, language-consciousness, or speech-thought — produces a remarkable similarity between languages. "There is something," says Lewis, "either in the structure of the mind or in the things it thinks about, which can produce the same results under very different conditions."[4] In man's earliest history, and in different places, cultures, and times, there were equations between sensibles and insensibles — good and happy with high and light, evil and pain with deep and dark, breath with soul, among others. Of these equations, Lewis says: "It is the very nature of thought and language to represent what is immaterial in picturable terms. . . . To ask how these married pairs of sensibles and insensibles first came together would be great folly; the real question is how they ever came apart."[5]

But come apart they did, and with the progress of analytical, discursive thinking an almost impassable barrier has been erected between sensibles and insensibles, the literal and the metaphorical, the intellectual and the imaginative, the phenomenal and the noumenal. The epistemological dichotomy is reflected in modern language which, among its many uses, improves the efficiency of language in two alternative directions — represented on the one hand by philosophic and scientific language, and on the other by poetic language (by which Lewis means imaginative language whether in prose or verse).

Scientific-philosophic language reduces an experience from a qualitative sensation into a manipulatable quantity, and in science escapes from the sensuous into a world of pure quantities, the ideal limit being represented by pure mathematics. Scientific language, in order to assert facts (i.e., predict experiences) must infer, and inference requires abstraction. The abstractions of science are not "real things" in the popular sense of having concrete embodiment in particular trees, flowers, animals, or other objects. Poetic or imaginative language, however, deals with concrete things we meet in real life — "things unique, individual, lovely, or hateful." Poetic language expresses by extralogical elements the very quality of an experience which scientific-philosophic language neglects.

The difference between the two types of language is not that one utters truth and the other fancy; they should be complementary. Science answers the question *whether* a thing exists; poetry answers *what* a thing is like. The scientific *whether* of existence is concerned with truth or fact; the poetic *what* of existence is concerned with meaning. For this reason, Lewis says, "Reason is the organ of truth; imagination is the organ of meaning."

Our modern epistemological divorce is that philosophic language fails to reach the concrete, and poetic language cannot prove the existence of anything. Lewis speculates that if creatures above us exist in the universe, their language would possibly represent the primitive unity of our own, so that "they can always in the same breath demonstrate *that* a thing is and present to you *what* it is." [6] Lewis often speculated that only on earth is there a distinction between imagination and reason, myth and fact.

Lewis did not limit the qualitative concern of imaginative

thought and language to the sensible world. He regarded the invisible, transcendent, supernatural world as equally real and concrete; as a matter of fact, he thought of ultimate reality as being, in the Platonic sense, too concrete for words. His point is that because of the necessity for reason to abstract, as in science and philosophy, the concretely real — whether in the sensible, insensible, or transcendent world — is closed to reason. Particularly is this true of transcendent reality, which must now be grasped by the imagination if it is to be grasped at all.

Imagination: The Organ of Meaning

Lewis calls imagination "the organ of meaning," a definition that initially appears so simple and yet is elusive and complex. Imagination may use the fundamental equivalence between sensibles and insensibles in two ways: allegorically (with allegory being related to metaphor and conceptual thought) or symbolically (with symbolism being related to mythology and nonconceptual thought). Allegory creates *visibilia*, usually fictional personifications, to express immaterial facts, emotions, and passions. Symbolism, however, views the material world as a copy, a frigid outline, of the unimaginable dimensions of the real invisible world. Allegory leaves the given, the immaterial world, for less real personifications; symbolism leaves the given, the material world, for the more real invisible world.

At root the distinction between allegory and symbolism is the difference between conceptual and nonconceptual thought. Lewis states: " In Allegory the images stand for concepts (giant Despair, Mr. Legality), in Symbolism for something the poet has experienced but which he has not reduced, perhaps cannot reduce, to a concept. Allegory can always be translated back into the concepts: the ' meaning' of a symbolical work cannot be stated in conceptual language because it is too concrete." [7] The profound difference between allegory and symbolism must not be forgotten. Allegory is clear and unambiguous, and there is a rough one-to-one relationship between the verbal symbol and the thing signified. The allegorist knows clearly what he is saying. But symbolism reaches "after some transcendental reality which the forms of discursive thought cannot contain." [8] Therefore Lewis makes the distinction, which we will now develop: "Symbolism is a mode of thought; but allegory is a mode of expression." [9]

Mythology: Grasping the Nonconceptual. Mythology, in Lewis' judgment, is the highest form of symbolism and can be grasped only by the imagination. Through mythology the imagination has an immediate nonconceptual apprehension of reality, grasps what baffles the intellect, and sees what reality is like in a more central region. The validity of the mythopoeic imagination is not open to reason's examination, for mythological images strike roots far beneath the surface of the mind, as though one had broken out of his normal mode of consciousness. The value of myth is independent of words or a particular literary work, and is found in a particular pattern of events that impresses itself on the imagination. When the events have been lodged in our imagination, the means of communication may be thrown away.

Basically there are two sources of myths. Out of the anthropological history of the race and emerging from the ranks of primitive myths, many of which are cruel, silly, and obscene, grow the great myths — Orpheus, Demeter and Persephone, the Hesperides, Balder, Ragnarok, and others. Then there are myths invented by individuals in fully civilized periods — such as the plots of *Dr. Jekyll and Mr. Hyde*, Wells's *The Door in the Wall*, Kafka's *The Castle*, or Tolkien's *The Lord of the Rings*. Of the modern myths, Lewis judges Macdonald's to be the best.

Lewis most fully discusses his understanding of myth in *An Experiment in Criticism*. For Lewis, the myth is extraliterary: its pattern can be contained in inferior words or told by different authors. It produces a permanent object of contemplation and conveys a peculiar flavor or quality, much as a smell or musical chord, and does not rely on the narrative attractions of suspense or surprise. The myth minimizes human sympathy so that, while we see the characters moving as shapes in another world and feel their profound relevance to our own life, we do not project ourselves into the characters. Myths make us sympathetic, not with the characters but with all men. Myth is always fantastic, dealing with impossibles and preternaturals. Though a myth may be sad or joyful, it is always grave. The myth is awe-inspiring and conveys a sense of the numinous that is greater than our conceptualization.

Lewis does not speculate about the ultimate origins of myths in prelogical minds or in the prehistory of the unconscious. Rather he is concerned with the impact that certain myths have on the imaginations of logical minds. The quality of the best myths is "the quality of the real universe, the divine, magical, terrifying and ecstatic reality in which we all live."[10] The key is that the experience of the highest reality is qualitative, as he says, "more like an adjective than a noun," not too vague and indefinable, but too concrete, real, and opaque for words.

Since the value of a myth depends on the one who hears or reads it, a story may be a myth for one man and not for another. But the story that does become myth for an individual claims the lasting allegiance of the imagination. The only verification of the truth of mythology is the deep, self-authenticating conviction that in the imaginative experience one has encountered reality, reality that cannot be defined, put into words, or grasped by the intellect. Lewis was convinced of what Ransom discovered in his space travels, "that the triple distinction of truth from myth and both from fact was purely terrestrial."[11] Since what appears as mythology on earth might appear as fact elsewhere in the universe, "our mythology is based on a solider reality than we dream."[12] Only the mythopoeic imagination can grasp this solid, concrete reality that has too many meanings to be reduced to concepts and words. Only the imagination can see the ancient unity and correspondence of things. Lewis' view of mythology has great importance for his approach to Biblical hermeneutics, which we shall examine shortly.

Metaphor: Supplying the Tools of Reason. The second approach of imagination to the equivalence of sensibles and insensibles is metaphorical and allegorical, the way of conceptualization. Although metaphor is a verbal symbol and allegory is a mode of expression, they both conceptualize experience by representing the immaterial in picturable terms. In fact, says Lewis, "every metaphor is an allegory in little."[13] Allegory creates *visibilia*, images, which are usually personifications, that have a rough one-to-one relationship to the invisible realities — facts, emotions, passions, concepts, the inward world — they represent. Later we shall explore Lewis' use of allegory as a literary form.

Our immediate interest is in the metaphorical aspect of imagination's conceptualizing function — the creation of verbal symbols that are indispensable to human reasoning. Without the prior work of the imagination, discursive reasoning is impossible. The power of reason is limited by the necessity of using language to think and to communicate thought. Language is inescapably metaphorical, increasingly so as it moves from pointing to particular sensible objects to speaking about causes, relations, mental states or acts. Lewis contends: "We apprehend none of these things except through metaphor. . . . Our only choice is to use the metaphors and thus to think something, though less than we could wish; or else to be driven by unrecognized metaphors and so think nothing at all."[14] The claim to independence of metaphor usually means the freedom to choose between one metaphor and another or, worse, to have words that contain an unrecognized metaphor.

Although reason deals with truth or falsity, it depends on the imagination that supplies, either by creating new metaphors or by revivifying old, the metaphorical tools essential to language and reason. Since all truth won by reason's use of metaphors can be no greater than the truth of the metaphors themselves, the validity of reason almost demands the validity of imagination. Imagination therefore is the organ of meaning, "meaning which is the antecedent condition both of truth and falsehood, whose antithesis is not error but nonsense." Thus the imagination is not the cause but the condition of truth. But Lewis warns that he is not "in any sense putting forward the imagination as the organ of truth." [15] He says, "I am a rationalist." Reason deals with truth or falsity. And part of the function of the imagination is to supply the linguistic tools for the rigorous dialectic of reason.

Reason: The Organ of Truth

In the realm of truth and fact, Lewis was a rationalist. Convinced of the "reasonableness" of Christianity and the validity of reason, Lewis is quite willing to subject the Christian faith to the examination of reason. Not only is he willing, but he insists that it be done. In fact, rational argument moves the struggle onto God's battleground. So Screwtape warns Wormwood not to argue with his "patient," but rather to keep a dozen incompatible philosophies dancing around in his head; to avoid asking whether a question is proved or disproved, but rather to ask whether it is "academic" or "practical," "outworn" or "contemporary." "Jargon, not argument," says Screwtape, "is your best ally." Once reason is awake, Screwtape worries, "who can foresee the result?" [16]

The Spirit of the Age wishes to use and not to use logical argument. Our contemporary glib and shallow rationalism, no longer schooled in the rigorous dialectic of logic, seeks the spirit of "free inquiry." Cold and objective nineteenth-century rationalism knew when an argument was proved or disproved, and the purpose of inquiry for them was to attain truth. Contemporary rationalists so enjoy the questing that they have forgotten the point of the quest. In *The Pilgrim's Regress*, Lewis satirizes the misuse of reason by various forms of rationalism — in science, Freudianism, the "reasonableness" of the cultured world, liberal Christianity, and the halfway house of idealism. Various forms of modern rationalism and naturalism want to use reason to "debunk" their opponent's argument, but do not want reason applied to their own arguments. Lewis is ready to follow reason to its logical end, in his own arguments and in those of his opponents. He scorns the easy "tolerance" that rests content with relative "honest opinions, sincerely expressed." As he says in *The Great Divorce*, "Thirst was made for water, inquiry for truth." [17] Or as Hingest tells Mark in *That Hideous Strength*: "There are a dozen views about everything until you know the answer. Then there's never more than one." [18]

Reason affords the only safe approach to contemporary naturalists, because the validity of reason is the only claim they cannot deny without cutting their own throats. If naturalists regard their views as being true, then they must admit the validity of reason; if with consistency they do not regard their views as true, then reason cannot approach them. But if they claim validity for their own arguments, as most of them do, then they must examine the Christian's or Platonist's or absolute idealist's arguments according to the rules of logic. That bit of inconsistency opens the door for reason. And here is the claim Lewis makes for it.

All knowledge, both theoretical and practical, depends on the validity of reason. This is true in morality, science, and philosophy. The validity of reason, including the principles of Practical Reason and the axioms of Theoretical Reason, is self-evident and neither demands nor admits proof. Lewis contends that "an open mind about the ultimate foundations either of Theoretical or of Practical Reason is idiocy." [19]

Accepting the validity of reason as self-evident, Lewis judges human rationality to be " the little tell-tale rift in Nature which shows that there is something beyond or behind her." [20] His logic is that just as individual human reasoning requires a rational cause to be valid, so the whole process of human reasoning requires a rational cause to be valid. No theory that explains human reason or mind as a result of irrational causes is admissible. But naturalism does just that. It holds that mind emerges from the Total System just like everything else, and that it is determined by the chance fluctuations of irrational atoms. Thus even the thought of the naturalist, produced by the same irrational causes, cannot be presented as valid; to do so would require a valid argument that no argument is valid, a proof that there are no proofs — which is nonsense. Reason, then, is independent of and not produced by nature, but does not exist absolutely on its own. The chain of rational causation must stop ultimately at a Self-existent Reason on which all reason depends. Thus it follows that the universe is ultimately mental and our logic is a "participation in the cosmic Logos." Mind is the principle behind the universe and the guarantor of the validity of reason. Only this kind of "mental" approach to the universe can encompass all the facts, which includes the fact of thinking itself. Only the a priori validity of reason can permit the possibility of talking about truth or falsity.

Because reason participates in the cosmic Logos, Lewis believes the weight of logical argument is on the side of the Christian apologist. Significantly, it is Reason in *The Pilgrim's Regress* who frees John from the prison of the Spirit of the Age. Admittedly, when opponents have carefully engaged in logical dialectic, they might not agree, but at least they will not talk nonsense. Most opponents of the Christian faith, however, resist ruthless logic. They are dabblers in philosophy and shallow reasoners who collect evidence and arguments favorable to themselves but ignore contrary evidence and logical consistency. So when Oyarsa tries to reason with Weston, Weston replies: "I don't pretend to be a metaphysician. I have not come here to chop logic." [21] Reason is the best tool for exposing question-begging arguments and superficial reasoning, challenging false systems, and pointing toward a theistic position.

As a rationalist, Lewis believes that reason faithfully pursued is a path that leads to God. Reason helps to clarify one's immortal longings and, when rigorously followed, can lead to a theistic position, and then to revelation and the door of faith. When properly used, reason is a humble master that has self-imposed limitations. Having arrived at the boundaries of its own domain, reason points to the church and to Christian experience. It is Reason, with sword drawn, that prevents John's retreat from Mother Kirk. Reason has led to the church but can go no farther. Lewis believes the statement that only he who does the will of the Father will know that the true doctrine is philosophically accurate. Reason could only lead to the abyss of abstraction. Reason knows that it cannot supply materials for correcting abstractions, so it is reason who says to go and try experience.

This is not to say, however, that one is to decide without evidence. On that Lewis repeatedly insists. " I am not asking anyone," he writes, " to accept Christianity if his best reasoning tells him that the weight of evidence is against it." [22] Reason has a duty not to decide without evidence and to speak only when it has made up its mind. We do not initially ask a man to believe in the doctrines of Christianity against his reason's best judgment. And that brings us to the relation between faith and knowledge, and to Lewis' somewhat unusual approach to the problem.

Faith and Knowledge

Lewis has been criticized for defining a Christian as " one who accepts the doctrines of Christianity." However, many of his critics do not read his total statement and miss his meaning. He defines Christian in this way because language must be used so that we can understand what is being said, and because a deeper or more spiritual definition is useless since we cannot judge another man's heart. He distinguishes two levels of faith: the first, intellectual assent to propositions; the second, trust in a person. Lewis borrowed the distinction without the terminology from Thomas Aquinas. Aquinas distinguished *fides*, intellectual assent to a proposition, from *fiducia*, the trust in another person, and contended that *fiducia* is not essential to salvation.

The distinction is important in the relation of faith, reason, and knowledge, and in the degree that knowledge is contained in faith. For Lewis, there is no conflict between faith and reason, and reason plays a role on both levels of faith. But on each level, faith exists only in the absence of demonstrable certainty. We never use the word " believe " for things we have found out, which is true for the scientist as well as for the Christian. The scientist labors, by testing hypotheses, to escape from belief into knowledge. Some Christians, of course, claim to have demonstrative proof, but if they did, they would not be believing but knowing. Degrees of religious and nonreligious belief vary from weak opinion to the kind of subjective certitude (the Christian's " I believe " and the atheist's " I don't believe ") that is untroubled by lack of demonstrative certainty. "Belief, in this sense," says Lewis, " seems to me to be assent to a proposition which we think so overwhelmingly probable that there is a psychological exclusion of doubt, though not a logical exclusion of dispute." [23] Many of our beliefs other than theological are held with more certitude than the evidence, if weighed in a laboratory manner, would justify.

On this first level of belief, of assent to certain propositions, all degrees of belief and disbelief are based on the assessment of reasonable evidence. And there is evidence for and against Christianity that rational minds, working honestly, can assess differently. To accept or to reject the Christian faith does not necessarily indicate unreason either way, only error. Lewis never asks a person to believe without evidence or in the face of evidence. All Christian believers, however, think they have good evidence, whether of metaphysical argument, history, religious experience, or authority. Reason evaluates the evidence and leads to the door of faith. In fact, Lewis could at this level of assent to the propositions of the Christian faith almost say with Aquinas that faith is an act of reason.

The attempt to live by this initial rational faith leads on to the higher level of faith. In trying and failing to practice the Christian virtues, the intellectual believer discovers that everything in life is a gift from God, and thus comes to trust God to do for him what he cannot do for himself. He discovers his moral and spiritual bankruptcy. At this point he goes beyond the propositions to God, from the logic of speculation to the logic of personal relations, from an argument that demands our assent to a Person who demands our confidence. The logic of personal relations alters the role of reason and the use of evidence. At this level of belief the Christian regards it as meritorious to adhere to his belief against any contrary evidence whatever.

Although the strength of our original assent does not by psychological necessity require such "obstinacy in belief," reason can show that the content of our faith indicates that such behavior is appropriate. If God is a beneficent being whose knowledge of our needs far exceeds our own, it logically follows that his actions will often appear to us as far from beneficent and wise. And observation teaches us how greatly the emotions, one's physical condition, one's wishes and desires and changing moods, affect one's spiritual life. Indeed, Christians have been warned that "trials to faith" and "temptations to doubt" would occur and that evidence strong enough to deceive the very elect will appear.

Our only consolation is that at times we seem to receive some favorable evidence for our faith, sometimes in the form of external events, at other times (however imperfect and intermittent) something like personal acquaintance with God, as well as the collective testimony of Christendom. Also we can understand that a personal relationship involves loving trust (sometimes in the teeth of contrary evidence), and that room for doubt is necessary for trust to grow. Christianity does not involve belief in "God," but belief in *this* God who confronts us as a Person and demands our confidence.

This demand for our faith in the face of evidence is two-edged and ambiguous. The same demand could be made by a trickster as well as a friend, by a delusion as well as God. To be forewarned against contrary evidence is rational if our belief is true; but if our belief is a delusion, it renders the delusion incurable. But that ambiguity alone makes faith possible — to be aware of the possibilities of delusion and yet reject them. In Lewis' view, Jesus did not rebuke the skeptic inquiring whether God exists, but the psychological quality of being "suspicious" in one who had long known a particular Person.

Thus the skeptic may dispute with the Christian on the grounds of his original assent, but not after he enters into relations with God. No longer can the Christian's belief be proportioned to every fluctuation of apparent evidence, or moods, or imagination, or even objecting reason. For even reason will at times say to the believer that Christianity appears to be highly improbable. Faith then, in Lewis' view, is not accepting Christianity in the face of evidence; but after reason has accepted Christianity, faith is holding on to it when doubts arise. At times, when a person is in a mood of despair, Christianity might look highly improbable. And Lewis himself was aware of the undulations of the spiritual life, of the dark nights of the soul, of the prayers that seem to be soliloquies, of the unanswered questions of human existence, of the dry periods when the Christian continues to act as if he believes, though his belief has fled. He had experienced what Screwtape warned Wormwood about: " Our cause is never more in danger than when a human, no longer desiring, but still intending, to do our Enemy's will, looks round upon a universe from which every trace of Him seems to have vanished, and asks why he has been forsaken, and still obeys." [24]

Thus faith in God can never reach the level of demonstrable certainty and knowledge. Nor would it be desirable. Faith must run certain risks, face the possibility of delusion, and still believe. For most people, faith cannot even permanently attain a psychological exclusion of doubt. The doubts will come. The ebb and flow of the spiritual life will occur. When they do, faith and reason, by long discipline, must control the Christian. In spite of moods, emotions, and doubts, the disciplined Christian continues to believe until his faith again revives and rises from the ashes. The obstinacy in belief occurs because of his encounter, however imperfectly or intermittently, with God. That the unbeliever cannot understand. " They cannot be expected to see how the *quality* of the object which we think we are beginning to know by acquaintance drives us to the view that if this were a delusion then we should have to say that the universe had produced no real thing of comparable value and that all explanations of the delusion seemed somehow less important than the thing explained. That is knowledge we cannot communicate." [25]

HERMENEUTICS: THE SCIENCE OF BIBLICAL INTERPRETATION

The value of Lewis' approach to hermeneutics is that of seeing how an "outside expert" deals with the problems of a specialized discipline, as he applies literary principles developed outside of the theological arena to the critical problems of Biblical interpretation. As a foremost literary critic and expert in ancient and medieval-renaissance literature, Lewis was intimately acquainted with the problems of the immediate and ultimate sources of ideas, and of the writing, transmission, and interpretation of literature.

His hermeneutical approach, which consists of some obvious faith presuppositions as well as some valuable scholarly insights, is a strange hybridization which fully satisfies hardly anybody. The limits he sets to Biblical criticism, his rejection of historical skepticism, his retention of mythopoeic language, and his ignorance of some elementary critical problems combine to draw fire from the higher critics. Yet his recognition of the absence of a theological system, of the mythological and metaphorical elements, and of error and inconsistency in the Bible causes uneasiness among fundamentalists and conservatives. There are values and weaknesses in Lewis' approach. We can profit from both. We will examine his general hermeneutical principles, his attitude toward Bibical criticism, and his method of interpreting the Biblical language.

General Principles

Transposition. The most important principle for Lewis, and what may be one of his most important contributions to theological thinking, is the concept of transposition. Developed at length in the sermon "Transposition," [26] the idea recurs repeatedly in his writings whenever he assumes that "the highest

THE FOUNDATION OF APOLOGETICS 85

does not stand without the lowest." The idea of transposition springs from the obvious fact of the continuity between natural and spiritual things, the fact that throughout nature transposition or adaptation exists whenever one goes from a lower to a higher or a higher to a lower medium.

Numerous cases of transposition can be found throughout nature. For example, in the relation of emotion and sensation, either joy or anguish may cause the identical physical sensation; but it would be absurd, because they produce the same sensation, to claim that joy and anguish are the same. The lower physical medium is limited and must use the same sensation to express quite opposite emotions. Or, the adaptation of an orchestral work into a piano arrangement requires that the piano represent different instruments with the same notes. Or in drawing, the three-dimensional world must be transferred to a two-dimensional surface. In all these instances, it is quite apparent that different evaluations can be made of the same event, depending upon whether it is viewed from above or below. If one approached these instances from below, one would see only a sensation, only notes on a piano, and only lines on a two-dimensional surface. It would be difficult to convince the observer that these were only impoverished representations of higher and richer realities. Yet the translation from a richer into a poorer medium is algebraical and not arithmetical, requiring that inadequate symbols or sensations must represent more than can be contained within themselves.

The concept of transposition is important for religion. The fact that religion uses natural language, acts, and emotions always provides prima facie evidence to its critics that it is nothing more than natural. Christians furnish heaven with terrestrial content; devotions borrow the language of erotic love; the symbol of the mystical union with Christ is the familiar act of eating and drinking. Lewis readily grants that religious language and imagery, the sacraments, and probably religious emotion too, contain nothing that has not been borrowed from nature. Yet looked at from above, we see that these transpositions attempt to embody the Christian life in the world, and that we are "trying to use natural acts and images and language with a new value." [27]

The concept of transposition finds wide application in Lewis' thinking. He thinks that it throws new light on the relation between mind and body, on the taking of humanity into God in the incarnation, and on the resurrection of the body and the life everlasting. It is basic for his approach to hermeneutics, where he thinks that the myths and rituals of nature religions are the inadequate expression in a lower medium of the truth that finally became incarnate in Jesus Christ. Scattered throughout nature are patterns that are flimsy reflections of higher truth. The cosmic pattern of redemption — of birth, death, and rebirth; of descent and reascent — is found embedded in the natural processes of the sun rising and setting, of the seasons, of the birth, death, and rebirth of the crops. For this reason Jesus is much like the Corn-King of pagan religion, but that is "because the Corn-King is a portrait of Him." The similarity is neither unreal nor accidental. There is a continuity of nature and spirit that is sacramental. Here, then, is a key principle: "the power of the Higher, just in so far as it is truly Higher, to come down, the power of the greater to include the less. Thus solid bodies exemplify many truths of plane geometry, but plane figures no truths of solid gometry: many inorganic propositions are true of organisms but no organic propositions are true of minerals." [28]

The inclusion of the natural by the spiritual is important, for the highest does not stand without the lowest. And the highest is not other than, but more than, the lowest, "as a flower differs from a bulb or a cathedral from an architect's drawing." [29] Transposition thus illuminates the connection of the Christian religion with pagan religion, ritual, and mythology, and shows how natural acts, emotion, and language can be transposed into vehicles of divine revelation. The man who looks at Christianity from below would see only an extension of the natural, and nothing more, just as a Flatlander could

THE FOUNDATION OF APOLOGETICS 87

see nothing but flat shapes in a picture. He sees all the facts, but not the meaning. Yet viewed from above, the transposition and retention of the lower medium is seen and the higher meaning recognized. The idea of transposition can serve a profound theological purpose in helping us understand how ultimate truth can use poorer vessels in being communicated to man.

Revelation. Lewis assumes that God is the Source of all truth, and that God has revealed himself in various ways in different places. Through the conscience, dreams, myths, the moral law, the election of Israel, the creation of immortal longings, and other ways, a divine pressure has been exerted on the mind of man. The purer elements of an Akhenaten, a Socrates, a Plato, or a Vergil contain divine truth. The monotheism of Akhenaten, for example, could have been an element in the Egyptian wisdom in which Moses was raised. At times the revelation comes unconsciously to men of insight, and later the old ideas take on a different meaning than they had for those who first said them. As Keble said, " Thoughts beyond their thoughts to those high bards were given." Ancient men of insight, both Biblical and pagan, at times said more than they knew, and meant more than they said. For example, from his knowledge of life and man and prompted by the recent death of his master Socrates, Plato imagines a perfectly righteous man who is treated as a monster of wickedness, and is bound, scourged, and impaled on a stake. Plato is consciously talking about the fate of goodness in a wicked world. But that was the discovery of an element of human experience of which the death of Christ is the supreme illustration. If Plato could have witnessed the death of Christ, he would have thought, " So that was what I was really talking about." [30] In the same way the Hebrew prophets were able to utter prophecies that had unconscious secondary meanings which became applicable to particular situations they had not specifically anticipated. Because he applies to himself passages that initially had other application, Jesus himself commits us to the principle of recognizing secondary meanings in the Scripture.

Thus, truth is truth, for Lewis, wherever it is found. If God enlightens every man, then indeed some pagans have glimpses, even if perverted, of truth; and it is natural to assume that some pagan truth may have influenced the Biblical people. By his catholic view of truth, Lewis avoids the much-discussed problem of the Hebrew and/or Greek origins of the Christian faith. Whatever truth entered the thinking of the church, it was guided by God. Whatever concepts, terms, titles, or religious myths and patterns became vehicles for the Christian faith, they were prepared by God during the history of revelation in view of the incarnation. The time and place of his incarnation were selected because then and there the elements existed that God had developed for that very purpose. Lewis argues: " For if we once accept the doctrine of the Incarnation, we must surely be very cautious in suggesting that any circumstance in the culture of first-century Palestine was a hampering or distorting influence upon his teaching. Do we suppose that the scene of God's earthly life was selected at random? — that some other scene would have served better? " [31]

Inspiration. Lewis has a broad view of inspiration. Not only were the Biblical writers inspired of God, but the Jews and the Christians who preserved and canonized the writings, and the redactors and editors who modified them, also had a divine pressure exerted on them, whether consciously or unconsciously, so that the end product, the Holy Scripture as we have it, is inspired of God. But it is important to note what Lewis means by this. Not all the Scripture is inspired for the same purpose or in the same way. As a literary man, Lewis was aware of the varied literary genres and the mixed elements in the Scripture. He was aware of the errors, contradictions, and sub-Christian ideas. By inspiration he does not mean that every sentence of the Old Testament, for example, has scientific or historical truth. He views The Book of Job or the story of Jonah as unhistorical and the early stories of Genesis as mythical. But this says nothing about their spiritual truth. Lewis is convinced that the writers have been guided by God.

The idea of transposition influences Lewis' view of inspiration. He believes that "the Scriptures proceed not by conversion of God's word into a literatuure but by taking up of a literature to be the vehicle of God's word." [32] The Scripture, as with all other instances of transposition, may be viewed either from above or from below. It is possible to view it from below and fail to see the upgrading and to regard the Scripture only as human literature. Or it may be approached from above and viewed, with all its imperfections and human content and retention of the lower medium of literature, as the vehicle of the Word of God. This requires "not merely knowledge but a certain insight; getting the focus right." [33] It would be as impossible to prove to a person without this insight that the Scripture is inspired as it would be to prove to an audience that could not read that a poem is more than black marks on white paper.

Though taken up and used in a higher way, the human literature remains, with all its weaknesses and imperfections. Nowhere in the Bible is there "unrefracted light giving us ultimate truth in systematic form." The Old Testament, for example, contains materials which are the same sort as those in other literature — chronicle, moral and political diatribes, poems, romances, myths — but which in different ways are burdened with a new privilege in the service of God's Word. But all the raw materials show through — the naïveté, error, contradiction, and even wickedness. Even in the teachings of Jesus, in which there is no imperfection, truth is not given in a cut-and-dried, foolproof, systematic form. He is an elusive teacher who hardly ever gives a straight answer to a straight question; his teachings are like trying to bottle a sunbeam. And concerning Paul, Lewis wonders why God, having given him so many gifts, withheld "that of lucidity and orderly exposition." So throughout the Scripture, spiritual truth can never by systematized, tabulated, memorized, and relied upon like a multiplication table. Lewis writes: "The total result is not 'the Word of God' in the sense that every passage, in itself, gives impeccable science or history. It carries the Word of God; and we . . . receive that word from it not by using it as an encyclopaedia or an encyclical but by steeping ourselves in its tone or temper and so learning its over-all message." [34] But because the Scripture is this way, we must conclude that in God's wisdom this is what is best for us at each level. So Jesus' teachings require us not to learn a subject but to become acquainted with a personality. The mixed contents of Paul's writings " finally let through what matters more than ideas — a whole Christian life in operation — better say, Christ operating in a man's life." [35]

Lewis did not believe in the infallibility or the verbal inspiration of the Scripture. He took seriously the progressive nature of God's gradual and graded self-revelation. He did not consider truth or value to be tied necessarily to historical or scientific accuracy. However, the value of some things — in particular the events of the incarnation — is inextricably bound up with their historical actuality. Lewis was convinced of the essential historical reliability of the New Testament, not in every detail but in its major thrust. One of the best indications of its reliability is the transparent honesty with which the writers placed apparently contradictory passages side by side. The best example of this, Lewis believed, is found in Mark 13:30–32, where Jesus predicts the second coming before the present generation had passed away, and then fourteen words later confessed that only the Father knows the time of the end. Side by side here is an exhibition of error and a confession of ignorance. " The evangelists," Lewis suggests, " have the first great characteristic of honest witnesses: they mention facts which are, at first sight, damaging to their main contention." [36]

It is clear now that Lewis did not indiscriminately or uncritically use the Scripture, but he did approach it with the assumptions that it is inspired of God, that the New Testament is in the main historically reliable, and that miracles can occur. His critical judgments were exercised within these guidelines, and for that very reason Lewis could never handle the Scripture in the ruthless manner of some modern critics who on other grounds have prejudged its historicity before they ever approach the Scripture.

Biblical Criticism

Lewis was often accused of being a fundamentalist. But many of his views, especially regarding the Scripture, are unacceptable to the fundamentalist. Lewis believed that the charge resulted from his refusal to hold an a priori prejudice against the miraculous or the supernatural which would predetermine his handling of the Biblical evidence. He tenaciously argued that he had never found any valid philosophic grounds for the universal negative proposition that miracles do not happen. Lewis has no built-in aversion to Biblical criticism. His reservations grow not out of an attempt to defend the infallibility of the Bible but out of reservations he holds as an expert literary critic. As a literary critic, he could see both the values and the limitations of Biblical criticism.

Lewis heartily endorsed the use of textual criticism and regarded it as a valuable apologetic tool in establishing the trustworthiness of the Biblical documents. He was, however, more skeptical of source criticism, particularly of the possibility of finding sources behind the sources, and felt that it is frequently led into error by the misuse of internal evidence. He was also skeptical about the possibility of dating texts too exactly on the basis of internal evidence. As a literary critic, he distrusted this mode of research.

Lewis said little about form criticism, but there is no doubt about his attitude. He recognized the changing forms, the accretions, and the conflicting versions of the same stories within the Scripture. But he opposed the excessive subjectivism and historical skepticism that is characteristic of some form critics, and he most certainly would have located the *Sitz im Leben* in the life of Jesus and not in the life of the church. He assumed that in general the writing, selection, and preservation of the

Scripture was done under the leadership of God.

The value of much Biblical criticism is vitiated, in Lewis' judgment, by our twentieth-century dearth of serious historical study. Chronological snobbery enslaves us to the modern climate of opinion, leads to unwarranted historical skepticism, and prevents an objective assessment of the Biblical records. Unexamined contemporary presuppositions often predetermine our evaluation of the Biblical data and repeatedly force us into the fallacy of begging the question. For example, Christ's apocalyptic outlook may be dismissed because he was influenced by the apocalyptic atmosphere of first-century Palestine. But that is to assume, without critical examination, that the apocalyptic expectation of a catastrophic end to the present universe is mistaken — which is begging the question. The same method may be employed in dating literature. For instance, it may be assumed that a book cannot be written before events to which it refers. The real problem would be whether predictions can occur. Or naturalistic presuppositions about the uniformity of nature can lead us to assume that miracles cannot happen, so that no amount of historical evidence can convince us that they have. Hume's traditional argument against miracle is that there is uniform experience against miracle; otherwise it would not be miracle. And that, Lewis argues, is a classic example of question begging. The authenticity of a particular Biblical miracle may be legitimately questioned, but not on the basis of an unexamined universal presupposition that miracles do happen.

Our perverted modern approach to history is most evident to Lewis in the historical "quests" of scholars. The severity of his judgment tempered with age, but in the 1940's he regarded the quests as a revolt against Christ, and he never ceased to regard the methods as unscholarly and the results as untenable. Extreme Biblical criticism began with an attack on Paul. Everything that nineteenth-century critics disliked about Christianity was attributed to Paul. He was supposed to have altered the kindly and simple teachings of Jesus into a cruel and

THE FOUNDATION OF APOLOGETICS

complicated religion — a view that is unimpressive to anyone who has carefully read the Gospels and the epistles; but, Lewis notes, apparently few people had, and the first victory was won.

The next step was an attack on the King himself under the guise of eliminating the accretions to and the perversions of his teaching, thereby getting back to the real Jesus. In this way the "historical Jesus" can be made to fit the preoccupation and prevailing ideas of any given contemporary situation. Once the historical existence of Jesus was doubted, and we were referred to vegetation myths and the mystery religions for the origin of the Christian faith. At one time Jesus was constructed on liberal and humanitarian lines. Later he can be pictured in Marxian, or revolutionary, or catastrophic terms. The earlier quests for the "historical Jesus" were seeking something that does not exist. Each quest must suppress the documents at one point and exaggerate at another. The same sort of guesswork produces a crop of new Napoleons, Shakespeares, and Swifts each year.

The current trend, as seen in scholars such as Rudolf Bultmann or J. A. T. Robinson or A. R. Vidler, is to eliminate not merely the accretions and perversions of Jesus' teachings but the transitorial, unessential archaisms of the Bible. Lewis warned against the dangers of this kind of subjective and skeptical approach from his first to his last book. Yet Lewis in his later years was more sympathetic with the desire of men like Vidler and Robinson to make the Christian faith relevant to the needs of modern man. But he disagreed with their methods of testing traditional doctrines and felt that their methods could not be consistently defended. Lewis wonders why the core of ideas and doctrinal beliefs that they retain might not one day be abandoned too. In Lewis' opinion, it is precisely the difficult problems that must not be eliminated. The deletion of archaisms and problem passages removes theological difficulties but at the same time provides no solutions or progress.

Several limitations of Biblical criticism can be summarily listed. (1) Do not uncritically judge the validity of ancient ideas by their concurrence with the ideas of our age; our own might be wrong. (2) Do not allow unexamined contemporary presuppositions to predetermine the handling of the Biblical texts. (3) Do not avoid the difficult problems or delete inconvenient data; that is the place to concentrate. (4) Do not butcher the Scripture by exaggerating some points and suppressing others; the documents say what they say.

The caution signs that Lewis planted in the path of Biblical criticism are valuable and, if followed, could help keep Biblical critics within bounds. But Lewis' refusal to acquaint himself with responsible Biblical criticism is almost inexcusable. His positive apologetic could have profited by knowing the best critical work. And he could also have avoided basing major arguments on what are at times very tenuous grounds. For example, Lewis did not apparently recognize the profound difference between the Johannine and Synoptic miracles. The critical problems are not at all alike in dealing with, say, the raising of Lazarus as compared with restoring the sight of Bartimaeus. Or take his basing the main argument for the historical accuracy of the New Testament on Mark 13:30-32. He seems unaware that the "Little Apocalypse" is among the most critically difficult of all New Testament passages, that it may be a confused collection of passages, part of which apply to the fall of Jerusalem and part of which apply to the Parousia. The present arrangement may not reflect the sayings of Jesus, only the understanding of the evangelist. The important thing is not that Lewis accept that critical judgment; but he most certainly should have been familiar with it. Virtually any modern commentary would have informed him of the problem.

Biblical Mythology and Metaphorical Language

Few topics have been more discussed by Biblical scholars in the past two decades than that of Biblical mythology and language. Rudolf Bultmann's 1941 essay "New Testament and Mythology," in which he advocates a radical demythologizing, precipitated the demythologizing controversy. Bultmann's intention was simply to make the gospel intelligible to the modern, scientifically-oriented man while preserving the essential *skandalon* of the gospel. It is generally granted that Bultmann is ambiguous and unclear, and that he includes as mythological certain events which others consider historical. Bultmann defines mythology as "the use of imagery to express the other worldly in terms of this world and the divine in terms of human life, the other side in terms of this side." The purpose of myth is not to present an objective picture of the world, "but to express man's understanding of himself in the world in which he lives."[87] But when Bultmann calls for demythologizing, it is not certain whether he means that the myth should be retained and interpreted or that myth is dispensable to religious expression.

Current theological discussion on demythologizing could profit by more exposure to Lewis' understanding of the mythopoeic nature of language, his theory of myth, and his understanding of the epistemological function of the imagination. It would not hurt theologians to listen to a great literary critic, an expert in linguistics, and one of the best-read men in mythology — Greek, Celtic, Nordic, Roman, and others. More than just talking or writing about mythology, Lewis loved and avidly read mythology throughout his life. His views thus convey some experiential insight.

We have already examined Lewis' view of myth in general. For him, mythology is more than merely man's use of imagery to picture the divine in terms of human life and to express his understanding of himself in the world in which he lives. Rather, mythological structures are inherent in the nature of reality, structures tied not to certain words but to certain patterns of events that impress themselves on the human imagination. The same patterns are found told in different words in widely separated places. The key to the whole cosmic drama — the central theme of life, death, and rebirth — is embedded in the myths of many races.

And that is not accidental. Myth is one of the means by which God reveals himself to mankind. Lewis believes that God is revealing himself in many ways and in many places. In *The Pilgrim's Regress* he develops the idea that God revealed himself to the Jews in the Law and to the pagans through myth. He believes that there is a divine call in pagan mythology, and that there is truth in the myths because they are valid, even if imperfect, imaginative glimpses of God. In terms of revelation, Lewis views myth at its best as "a real though unfocussed gleam of divine truth falling on human imagination."[38]

Consequently, Lewis could not contrast myth to fact, truth, or history. He does not think of myth as expressing the otherworldly in terms of this world (as does Bultmann), or as a symbolic representation of nonhistorical truth (as does Niebuhr). He thinks of Judeo-Christian myth more in the Socratic sense of "a not unlikely tale of what might have been historical fact,"[39] but which by all means is an imaginative glimpse of divine truth. Bultmann finds the sources of Christian myth in Jewish apocalyptic and Gnostic redemption myths, and *ipso facto* tends to discount their validity. Origin is irrelevant for Lewis because he assumes that God is revealing himself through myth, both pagan and Biblical, which explains the occurrence of ideas in pagan religion similar to those in the Christian faith. Assuming that Christianity is true, it could avoid some coincidence with other religions only if all other religions were one hundred percent false. Resemblances therefore say nothing either for or against the truth of the Christian faith.

Divine and diabolical and human elements all play a part in mythology. But the great pagan myths do contain glimpses of divine truth — whether in the transcendent monotheism of an Akhenaten, or the theistic leap of a Plato, or in the figures of the pagan Christs (Balder, Osiris, Adonis, etc.). The Jews also had their mythology, and because they were the chosen people theirs was the chosen mythology. There was a gradual focusing of mythology which culminates in myth becoming historical fact in the incarnation. In the New Testament, in contrast to Bultmann's view, history reigns supreme and truth becomes incarnate. Lewis says: "It is not an accidental resemblance that what, from the point of view of being, is stated in the form 'God became Man,' should involve, from the point of view of human knowledge, the statement 'Myth became Fact.'" [40] Here the concept of transposition is relevant. The highest myth, expressed in personal categories, rests on lower myth, expressed in natural categories. The highest does not stand without the lowest. The highest myth transposes the lower myth into another key without destroying the value of the earlier form.

An important point for Lewis is that although myth becomes fact in the New Testament, it still remains myth. "Just as God is none the less God by being Man, so the Myth remains Myth even when it becomes Fact. The story of Christ demands from us, and repays, not only a religious and historical but also an imaginative response. It is directed to the child, the poet, and the savage in us as well as to the conscience and to the intellect. One of its functions is to break down dividing walls." [41] This view is perfectly consistent with Lewis' epistemology which holds that reason grasps facts and imagination grasps meaning. The reason could comprehend all the facts of the incarnation without understanding its meaning. The truth that becomes incarnate in Jesus is more than we can think or say; it addresses our imaginations.

But here Lewis diverges drastically from Bultmann. Bultmann is unconcerned about *historie*, i.e., the facts of past experience. Truth for him is existential truth which addresses man in the kerygma. But history is important for Lewis. The incarnation is precisely myth becoming fact. The Christian story is about a historical personage. The vast and vague truth of myth and ritual focuses in a historical event in Palestine.

Lewis is also more restrictive than Bultmann in his definition of myth. When Bultmann views myth as describing "the other world in terms of this world," myth includes virtually everything in the Bible. He labels mythological such disparate elements as the prescientific world view, good and evil spirits, miracles, the salvation event, Christological concepts, the reality of the Holy Spirit, and eschatological concepts. Bultmann does not carefully distinguish between the use of metaphor, analogy, and myth; and he does not seem adequately to recognize the metaphorical nature of language.

Lewis, however, keeps in mind the distinctions between thought, imagination, and language; between a prescientific world view, mythical patterns, and metaphorical language. He is convinced that "man is a poetical animal and touches nothing which he does not adorn." [42] All language about things other than physical objects is necessarily metaphorical, including the language of science, philosophy, psychology, politics, or economics. The only difference is that metaphors in these specialized vocabularies often go unrecognized and are accepted as literal, thereby dominating their users. Thus we cannot restate our belief in a form free from metaphor and symbol. "We can make our language duller; we cannot make it less metaphorical." [43]

Limits must be set, however, as to what is and what is not metaphor. For Lewis the metaphorical language of the Bible concerns two things: "the supernatural, unconditioned reality, and those events on the historical level which its irruption into the natural universe is held to have produced." [44] Here Lewis makes an important distinction: We cannot make "literal" statements about God or eternal, unconditioned reality, but we can speak literally of events on the historical level. When we speak of God, or of Christ as God's Son, or of Christ's coming down or ascending to heaven, or of hell "fire," obviously we are speaking metaphorically. However, the assertion that Jesus turned water into wine is a perfectly literal statement which, if it happened, was well within reach of our senses and language. Explanation becomes muddled or dishonest when we try to interpret historical events metaphorically. The imagination may be required to grasp their full meaning, but not to establish that they occurred. Eternal truth is not empirically verifiable, but historical events are. And so the great incarnation events — the miracles, the cross, the resurrection — were within the bounds of sensory verification, and are therefore either lies, or legends, or history.

Can we then demythologize the language of the Bible to make it more intelligible to modern man? Lewis answers an emphatic "no." The historical events were empirically verifiable facts that cannot be demythologized or metaphorically interpreted. To demythologize supernatural, unconditioned reality requires that we remythologize in a poorer language. Admittedly, the Bible speaks of God with anthropomorphic images. But to relinquish the metaphor "Father" for abstract philosophic language is hardly an advancement. To speak of God as a "spiritual force" conjures up ideas of winds and tides, electricity and gravitation; as "the ground of being," ideas of an extended gas or fluid; as a "substance," ideas perhaps of tapioca pudding. To speak of Christ "entering the universe" rather than "coming down from heaven" only substitutes horizontal for vertical movement. Many advanced ways of thinking about God and religion are more absurd than the manlike images of the Bible and merely substitute a poorer for a richer mythology.

So Lewis opposes demythologizing while recognizing the mythological and metaphorical character of the Bible. Not only is demythologizing impossible, it is undesirable. For the import of the Biblical images is more trustworthy than our theological abstractions. Lewis suggests two rules for exegetics in regard to images: "(1) Never take the images literally. (2) When the *purport* of the images . . . seems to conflict with the theological abstractions, trust the purport of the images every time. For our abstract thinking is itself a tissue of analogies: a continual modelling of spiritual reality in legal or chemical or mechanical terms. Are these likely to be more adequate than the sensuous, organic, and personal images of scripture — light and darkness, river and well, seed and harvest, master and servant, hen and chickens, father and child? The footprints of the Divine are more visible in that rich soil than across rocks or slag-heaps." [45]

But what about the imagery that conflicts with our scientific knowledge? Here Lewis emphasizes the difference between thought, imagination, and speech. He devotes a whole chapter in *Miracles* to the distinction. He argues that correct thinking may be accompanied by false imagining, even when false images are mistaken for true ones. For example, a child might avoid poison while thinking of poison as "Horrible Red Things," in which case the child's thinking would be correct while his imagination was wrong. Similarly, the truth or validity of thinking in the Biblical insights is not tied necessarily to the literal truth of the Biblical images. Lewis argues that the Biblical people did not distinguish between the material and immaterial, between the image and the thing signified, to the same degree as modern men. And beyond the necessity of using metaphorical language, the early Christians indeed might have imagined that God lives in a sky palace and that Christ now sits at his right hand. But the images were not what mattered. They believed in God and used the only means at their disposal to express that belief. Any of them, if he had received an Alexandrian philosophical education and discovered the images to be false, would not have been disturbed. As soon as the distinction between the spiritual and the physical was before their minds, they knew God to be spiritual and realized that this had always been the implication of their religion.

Lewis provides a useful distinction in that of thought, imagination, and speech, and that of unverifiable eternal truth and verifiable historical events. Although there is value in the distinction, it nonetheless leaves Lewis with some difficult problems. What about the ascension, for example, an event on the borderline between fact and myth? His distinction between thought and imagination does not adequately explain this. It is true that the disciples were concerned with transcendence and the rulership of Christ, and that an Alexandrian education would have taught them that heaven is not a local habitat of God up in the sky. But to argue, as does Lewis, that whatever they saw, they would have remembered it as a vertical ascent, is to avoid the problem. The fact remains that the disciples either saw or did not see a bodily ascension, or that either they consciously expressed it mythologically or God absurdly gave a physical demonstration for their nonscientific minds. It becomes apparent that the borderline events of the incarnation — e.g., the resurrection and the ascension — cannot be neatly fit into the category of historically verifiable events. To make them *simply* empirically verifiable ignores the fact that in the New Testament records these events seem to have been open only to the eyes of faith.

And yet, Lewis does have a valid point that the miracles, the death, resurrection, and ascension are distinctly different from the Old Testament myths of the Creation or the Fall, or the New Testament metaphorical statements that call Jesus the " Son of God " or say that he " reigns at the right hand of God." But, in fairness, we must say that if Bultmann is guilty of eliminating too much history and fact in his demythologizing, Lewis is guilty of oversimplification and of an inexcusable neglect of the results of the best Biblical scholarship.

However, Lewis' approach to Biblical criticism offers a middle ground between radical criticism and literalism. Consequently, he can please neither the liberal nor the conservative. The value of his hermeneutic method is that he recognizes the mythological and metaphorical nature of much of the Biblical language without either minimizing its meaning or being led into historical skepticism. Lewis explains the metaphors without explaining away. He believes that the truth behind the metaphors of the cross, or hell " fire," or the Fall remains just as supernatural and shocking after their metaphorical nature is realized. But beyond this, Lewis believes that the Biblical images and symbols themselves are inspired of God and therefore should be retained and interpreted. The personal images of the New Testament especially must be retained, because the personal is the highest thing we know in human experience. They are more accurate than anything that can be substituted for them. Lewis argues that it is legitimate to leave the words of the

Bible to make a point clear. "But you must always go back. Naturally God knows how to describe Himself much better than we know how to describe Him." [46]

THEOLOGY: THE FORMULATION OF FAITH

Lewis repeatedly insisted that he was no theologian, and at crucial points he often submitted his ideas to the correction of "real theologians." Nevertheless, despite his rejection of the title, any person who has written the number of books on the Christian faith that Lewis has works from some definite theological presuppositions and expounds considerable theology. And he ought to know what he is talking about or abandon the effort. W. Norman Pittenger accused Lewis of being an inept theologian, and on occasion the accusation is valid. At times the subtleties of a problem are missed by Lewis, or he may misunderstand the meaning of a particular theological idea (e.g., his misunderstanding of "total depravity"), or his logic may go astray, or his stated alternatives do not exhaust the possibilities. But his posture of humility or his occasional lapse of insight should not lead to contemptuous dismissal of his theological competence. Indisputably, Lewis was widely read in theology — especially in the Fathers, Augustine, and Aquinas, as well as having more than passing acquaintance with scattered theologians throughout the history of the church. His greatest deficiency was in modern theology, although even here he had considerable knowledge of the major contemporary theologians. But his heart was in the past, and he was not impressed by current vogues or passing phases in theology. For his basic theological ideas he went to the Bible and to the central tradition of the church.

Nowhere does Lewis intend to be a theological innovator. His stated intention was to present "mere Christianity," traditional orthodoxy, which one encounters in different communions in widely separated centuries. When he deviates from that tradition, it is either unconsciously or for a good reason. He submitted the manuscript of Book II of *Mere Christianity* to four clergymen of different faiths (Anglican, Methodist, Presbyterian, and Roman Catholic) who with only two minor exceptions agreed with his thought. He desired to avoid theological controversy so that the essence of the Christian faith would be heard. And he deviated from that course only in his last writing, *Letters to Malcolm*, where he dealt with some controversial subjects such as liturgy, devotions to the saints, the Sacraments, and prayers for the dead. So in his writings one encounters very little that is new or that could not be found somewhere else, but in few places can one find old ideas presented in such scintillating fashion.

There is no systematic development of theology by Lewis, but scattered throughout his writings he deals with the main subjects of systematic theology. Lewis' theological ideas are difficult to categorize. One safe statement is that he would not be labeled a liberal. Any attempt to force his ideas into a system is artificial. This sketch of his theology will use the broad divisions of systematic theology only for the sake of convenience.

The Doctrine of God

At least three main concerns emerge in Lewis' doctrine of God. First, he wants to confront man with the Utterly Concrete Fact of existence, the God " who does one thing and not another, a concrete, choosing, commanding, prohibiting God with a determinate character," [47] the God who is the source of all concrete, individual things and events. Second, Lewis presents theism in contrast to pantheism and deism and consciously attempts to avoid those extremes. Third, he attempts to present a balanced view of God — of God as Love and Wrath, Remote and Near, Hidden and Revealed, Supreme Goodness and Supreme Terror — which is faithful to the Biblical witness and impresses the seriousness of man's alienation from him. The total effect is to place God as a commanding Fact in the midst of the arena of life, which brings Lewis into conflict with many modern views of God.

Several critics have accused Lewis of having a quasi-deistic view of God, but that charge is patently absurd.[48] Throughout his writings he assails both deism and pantheism. Against pantheism, he contends that the man who does not think of God as other than himself, an otherness to which there is no parallel, has no religion at all. Or, against deism, he argues that if we think of God as having a parallel or discontinuous existence to our own, in the same way as other men or objects in general, then we have made an idol. There is an ontological continuity between the Creator and his creatures. He writes: "There is here no question of a God 'up there' or 'out there'; rather, the present operation of God 'in here,' as the ground of my own being, and God 'in there,' as the ground of the matter that surrounds me, and God embracing and uniting both in the daily miracle of finite consciousness."[49] He explicitly rejects the idea of a Managerial God with his general laws, and views God as intimately involved with his creation. Far from quasi-deism, Lewis believes that everything is specially providential, and that the divine plan can be altered by an individual's prayer. The world is actually crowded with God, and though he often walks there incognito, the incognito is not difficult to penetrate. The world and its objects can become conductors of divine activity, and every situation to the awakened subject is a possible theophany. And so Lewis stresses both the transcendence and the immanence of God.

Our thinking about God must maintain a balance between metaphysical and theological abstractions and anthropomorphic images. The abstractions, which are negative in form (infinite, immaterial, impassible, immutable, etc.), result from the positive intuitions and visions of the great saints who pronounce that God transcends the limitations called materiality, personality, change, passion, and the like. The abstractions check a naïve reliance on anthropomorphic images, but can be dangerous if we regard them as the literal truth and use the negative abstractions unchecked by any positive intuition. Abstraction alone loses the living, acting God, and leaves man worshiping a pure abstraction, a nonentity. Therefore, because the personal is the highest reality we experience, Lewis retains the anthropomorphic images of the Bible and contends that these best convey the idea of the concrete, acting, judging, redeeming God of the Bible. He writes: "But never, here or anywhere else, let us think that while anthropomorphic images are a concession to our weakness, the abstractions are the literal truth. Both are equally concessions; each singly misleading, and the two together mutually corrective." [50]

There is no major new theological contribution by Lewis to the doctrine of God, but he does have some fascinating flashes of insight into the character of God. For example, in discussing God's omnipotence, he suggests that omnipotence does not mean that God can do anything; he cannot do what is intrinsically impossible or violates his nature or impinges on human freedom. Yet, in another sense, all *things* are possible; but "intrinsic impossibilities are not things but nonentities . . . nonsense remains nonsense even when we talk it about God." [51] Or again, he suggests that God's freedom is not an indeterminate choice between alternatives, but "consists in the fact that no cause other than Himself produces His acts and no external obstacle impedes them." [52] Or when he describes the love of God, he is opposing modern Christianity-and-water. The loving God is "not a senile benevolence that drowsily wishes you to be happy in your own way, not the cold philanthropy of a conscientious magistrate, nor the care of a host who feels responsible for the comfort of his guests, but the consuming fire Himself, the Love that made the worlds, persistent as the artist's love for his work and despotic as a man's love for a dog, provident and venerable as a father's love for a child, jealous, inexorable, exacting as love between the sexes." [53]

Whatever the theological finesse of his doctrine of God, having read Lewis, one finds it difficult to forget his metaphors and descriptions of God — of the God who is beyond the bright blur, the Great Iconoclast to our false images, the Jealous Lover who takes seriously his beloved, the God who must be sought for himself alone, whom to seek for any other reason is to lose him. Or he speaks of God as being " so brimful of existence that he can give existence away," [54] or as so filling the world and sanctifying its experiences that " pleasures are patches of godlight in the woods of our experience." [55] His God is pure act, not an impassible God; the God who takes sin seriously, who initiates a divine invasion into human history as the culmination of his self-revelation. He is the God who is so fully present that any moment or any experience is a possible theophany; and yet he is the hidden God who so often is absent in time of trouble, the God who at crucial times does not make himself known to his greatest saints.

Even this cursory survey of his idea of God shows a fertile mixture of theology, philosophy, freewheeling analogy, daring metaphor, honest skepticism, and devotional piety. It is a picture drawn by a man who was pursued by the Hound of Heaven, lured on toward the Supreme Good by *Sehnsucht,* who speaks boldly of what he has experienced and honestly admits the tentativeness of his unexperienced speculations. It is a picture drawn by a man who knows the danger and value of anthropomorphic images, but also the barrenness and vacuity of theological abstractions; who can distinguish between the Reality and the picture of the Reality. It is a picture drawn in relation to the pressing problems of pain and suffering, of the regularity of the natural order and miracles, of the longing for God in the human heart, of prayer and pleasures and human destiny. And if Lewis is right that we best think of God in images, then any person will have his experience enriched by the flood of divine images that rushes at him in the writings of Lewis.

Time and Eternity

An important idea for Lewis, which must be examined, is that God's mode of existence is timeless eternity, an Eternal Now, in which all historical events and moments enjoy simultaneity. This forms part of his solution to the problems of prayer, of God's sovereignty and human freedom of the will, of the incarnation, and of God's providence in the world. Thus prayers are answered in one sense before the foundation of the world, because all future historical moments and events were present in God's Eternal Now and our prayers were one of the factors God took into account in determining the destiny of the world. This explains why we can pray for events that must have been determined at the moment of creation or why a prayer offered at twelve o'clock may become part of the cause of an event happening at ten o'clock, if the results of the event are unknown to the one who prays. The idea of timeless eternity also eliminates the question of how the universe kept running when the Eternal Logos became incarnate, for the incarnation did not exist for God in terms of temporal succession. The idea of timeless eternity solves the problem of special providences within nature, because God takes all future factors into account in the act of creation. General providence and natural causation, in this view, are not alternatives, but are the same thing and determine every event.

The idea of timeless eternity is of crucial importance for Lewis' approach to numerous apologetic problems, and his arguments to some extent stand or fall with its validity. But the idea of timeless eternity is at best difficult to defend, is most certainly derived from Platonic and not Biblical thought, and suffers from what Lewis himself charges against many non-Christian ideas: it is too simple. It is a boy's approach to difficult problems. Lewis would have done well to read Oscar Cullmann or the later Karl Barth. Lewis' view of time and eternity is one of the weakest links in his apologetic chain, and, unfortunately, it is one of the most important.

The Doctrine of the Trinity

For Lewis, theology is based on the experimental knowledge of God as he reveals himself within the Christian community, meaning that the doctrine of the Trinity introduces the discussion of Christian theology.[56] We experience God in a threefold way. In prayer he is the One to whom we pray, the motive power within us pushing us on, and the road along which we are pushed. And our historical experience of God has been threefold: the God of the Jews, the Incarnate Lord, and the Spirit within the Christian church.

Lewis adheres to traditional trinitarian thought and accepts the Nicene and Chalcedonian Creeds, but conveys the complex trinitarian idea through simple analogies. Some criticisms of Lewis' treatment of the Trinity result from the critic isolating one analogy from the several he uses. One of his illustrations of the relation of the Son to the Father distinguishes between "making" and "begetting." To make or create is to make something other than and different from oneself. To beget is to create something out of oneself. So God makes men, but he begets the Son, and what he begets is God.

Lewis leans heavily on the social doctrine of the Trinity. Although he speaks of Father, Son, and Spirit as Persons who are yet beyond personality, he also refers to them as personalities. Only the use again of transposition spares him the danger of having personality interpreted in terms of individuality, which borders on tritheism. He means that they are personalities and yet are beyond personality, not in the sense of being other than personal but of being superpersonal. What we know on the human level as personalities are on the divine level taken up and combined in new ways. On the human level, one person and one being are coextensive; but on the divine level, One Being is Three Persons while remaining One Being, much as a cube is six squares while remaining one cube. A person living in two dimensions could not imagine a cube, yet three-dimensional space takes up and combines two-dimensional space in new ways. The analogy of a cube is inadequate by itself because it contains no personal dimensions. But in conjunction with his discussion of a social Trinity, the analogy of a cube helps illustrate the transposition of the personal to the superpersonal dimension on the divine level, the subsuming of the lower into the higher level.

God's love is the bond uniting the Three Persons in One Being. The statement "God is love" has no meaning unless God is at least two Persons, because love is something one person has for another. If God were a single Person, then before the world was made, he was not love. So the dynamic activity of love was going on before the world was made, and the love that grows out of the union of Father and Son is such a concrete, living thing that the union itself is also a real Person, the third of the three Persons who are God. God, then, is a community of life, of dynamic, pulsating activity, which Lewis best describes, if not irreverently, as a kind of drama or a dance.

The Person and Work of Christ

W. Norman Pittenger accused Lewis of having a docetic Christology, falling between Apollinarianism and Eutychianism, respectively between the idea of the Logos replacing the mind in a human body and that of the divinity swallowing up the humanity of Jesus — which only indicates that Pittenger selectively reads Lewis.[57] On the contrary, Lewis repeatedly emphasizes Christ's genuine humanity and the limitations of the incarnation, including ignorance. The real humanity, in fact, is probably the key to Lewis' Christology: the incarnation is God taking humanity up into himself. The Son is eternally begotten of the Father, but he lays aside his eternal powers and accepts human limitations in the incarnation. He becomes a new kind of man, in fact, *the* new man, the archetypal individual who includes redeemed humanity within himself and who becomes the interanimating Spirit of the new humanity. In this one instance humanity arrived and passed into the life of God, and, after being killed, "the Man in Christ rose again: not only the God."[58] The resurrection and ascension are the triumphs of man as well as the acts of God. Lewis places strong emphasis on the humanity of Christ in glory, the culmination of the taking up of man into God.

Lewis stands in the center of historic, conciliar Christological thought. He accepts at face value the Scriptural accounts of the virgin birth, the life and ministry, the death, bodily resurrection, and ascension of Jesus. This uncritical acceptance of the Scriptural account leads Lewis to set up his now famous, oft-repeated, Christological alternative. From the fact that Jesus claimed to be God and to forgive sins, Lewis argues that it is not possible to believe that Jesus was merely a great moral teacher. " That is the one thing we must not say. A man who was merely a man and said the sort of things Jesus said would not be a great moral teacher. He would either be a lunatic — on a level with the man who says he is a poached egg — or else he would be the Devil of Hell. You must make your choice. Either this man was, and is, the Son of God: or else a madman or something worse." [59] That is probably the single most quoted and assailed statement by Lewis. It has been accused of being crude, vulgar, naïve, dishonest, a shock tactic, and much else. Its very apparent weakness is that the logical coerciveness of the alternatives requires a prior affirmation of the Scriptural account that Jesus claimed to be God and to forgive sins. Unless the Scriptural account is accurate, there are many other good alternatives to the Christological question. But Lewis accepts the Scriptural account and utilizes its terms and concepts to describe the Son in his own writings.

The incarnation is the Author becoming an Actor in his own play. The Son of God is God stooping to conquer. He is the historic manifestation of the universal pattern of descent and reascent, of death and rebirth, of going down to go up. In the descending and reascending, " God dredged the salt and oosy bottom of Creation." [60] There is no docetism here. Matter and man, the whole creaturely predicament, are taken into God's own being. " So that 'He came down from Heaven' can almost be transposed into 'Heaven drew earth up into it,' and locality, limitation, sleep, sweat, footsore weariness, frustration, pain, doubt and death, are, from before all worlds, known by God from within." [61]

Jesus as the archetypal new man is pivotal in Lewis' understanding of the work of Christ. As the archetypal man, Jesus recapitulates the history of the race, and his death and resurrection become vicarious on behalf of man. He is the representative Die-er, the one who freely chose to become man, and as perfect man died the perfect death. The death is the key to the life of Christ and the means by which sin is forgiven. Theories about the death are secondary and not essential, and Lewis seems to utilize whatever is helpful in any theory. He describes Jesus as the Perfect Penitent. Repentance is not what God requires, but is simply a description of what going back to God is like: it is surrender, submission, dying, and receiving God into oneself. A man cannot repent perfectly. But the God-Man could. " He could surrender His will, and suffer and die, because He was man; and He could do it perfectly because He was God." [62] The death is also substitutionary, in the sense not of Christ's being punished but of God's " footing the bill " for man's sin. And the death was not an afterthought of God. " The Incarnation is not an episode in the life of God: the Lamb is slain — and therefore presumably born, grown to maturity, and risen — from all eternity." [63] Because vicariousness is at the heart of reality, Christ's higher and mystical death, which is in itself good and a necessary ingredient of the higher life, can become ours. By faith in him we die to live.

Man and Sin

Man, for Lewis, is God's grand enterprise, an organism that is also a spirit, a spiritual animal commanded to become a god. An amalgamation of Scriptural myth and scientific theory forms his view of man's origin and history. Modern science suggests that man physically descended from the animals and that the first men were brutes and savages. If no moral connotation is attached to the term " brute," then Lewis has no objection to the scientific view. But he cautions that crudity of artefacts or physical appearance says nothing about the intelligence or virtue of the first men. Evolutionary theories clearly posed no problem for Lewis' faith, though on occasion he indicated that he held some scientific reservations. Yet in the broader statement of his faith he seems to incorporate evolutionary theory into his thinking.

But Lewis balances his acceptance of man's continuity in the chain of physical development with the Bible's emphasis on man's uniqueness. At some point in the chain of animal development, God gave man the power of self-transcendence, the awareness of "I" and "Not-I," of God as his Creator, and the power of moral judgment — which opened for the creature the terrible alternative of choosing God or self as the center for his life. For Lewis, the Genesis stories are myths that embody the truth that man is made "out of" something else, that he is an animal raised to be more than an animal, and taken up into a new life without relinquishing the old life. The details of the Genesis stories are unimportant, but Lewis views them as conveying that the first men were completely good and happy. He speculates that Paradisal Man's new consciousness flooded his whole organism and was not limited just to his brain — a power of which the modern Yogi's is a mere reflection. Thus his will perfectly controlled his organic processes, his appetites, his waking and sleeping, and even the length of his life. As a prototype of the Christ who lived in conscious self-surrender to his Creator, he held God preeminent in his love and thought. He commanded all lower forms of life and was a priest mediating to them the splendors of God. Judged by his artefacts, appearance, or language, he would appear a savage. But despite his inability to conceptualize, he would have been capable of momentous spiritual experiences and moral living. Lewis says, in one of his famous statements: " I do not doubt that if the Paradisal man could now appear among us, we should regard him as an utter savage, a creature to be exploited or, at best, patronised. Only one or two, and those the holiest among us, would glance a second time at the naked, shaggy-bearded, slow-spoken creature: but they, after a few minutes, would fall at his feet." [64]

Lewis does not speculate about how many of these Paradisal men might have lived or how long the Paradisal state lasted.

But sooner or later Paradisal Man fell. And man as we now know him is a horror to God and himself, ill-adapted to the universe, and subject to death. He is in conflict with his organism, nature, and his fellowmen. He is bound up in self-will. Our present state was brought about by the Fall.

Lewis understands the Genesis myth of the Fall in the Socratic sense of "an account of what *may have been* the historical fact." [65] But the historical, psychological, and spiritual fact is not tied to the details of the Genesis account. It may or may not have had something to do with the eating of an apple. Both the importance of the Fall and the unimportance of the historical details are seen in Lewis' own different remythologizings of the myth of the Fall. In *The Problem of Pain* he patterns his myth of Paradisal Man in a garden closely after the Genesis story. In *The Pilgrim's Regress* he tells a myth of a tenant and his wife who live on a Landlord's farm in the middle of a park. In *The Magician's Nephew*, Digory's sinful curiosity precipitates the Fall. Lewis' most haunting remythologizing of Paradise and the Fall is in *Perelandra* where a King and Queen live in innocence in a Paradise on Venus. There the Un-man, who is the incarnation of evil, tempts the Green Lady, the Eve of Venus, to disobey God and leave the floating islands and stay overnight on the Fixed Island. The Fixed Island is a profound symbol for the desire to command the future and take it out of God's hands.

The very diversity of Lewis' myths of the Fall indicates that, whatever the particular act or series of acts, the Fall was prompted by Paradisal Man's desire to become a god, to mark off a corner of the universe for his own, to turn from adoration and obedience to God to himself. Pride, then, is the great sin, and all other sin flows out from it.

The result of the Fall "was the emergence of a new kind of man — a new species, never made by God, had sinned itself into existence." [66] Now God rules man more externally, not by laws of the spirit but by laws of nature. Man is subject to ordinary biochemical laws and has no control over desire, pain, senility, and death. His will no longer rules his organism; he has become a prisoner in his own house. His self is perverted. Man lost his original nature, his status as a species, and his spiritual organism lapsed back into a merely natural state.

This condition is transmitted by heredity to the race. Lewis does not speculate on how sin is transmitted, except to assert that mankind is corporately present in some way in great archetypal individuals like Adam or Christ. He is aware of the sense of social corporateness among the Jews and their apparent ignoring of our sense of the individual. He believes there is some kind of interanimation of humanity, not in the sense of the Patristic doctrine of our physical presence in Adam's loins, or Anselm's idea of inclusion by legal fiction, or in any metaphorical or causal sense, but in a deeper mystical fashion. Original sin is affirmed and actualized by the daily prideful choice by the individual of himself instead of God.

Lewis rejects the doctrine of total depravity "partly on the logical ground that if our depravity were total we should not know ourselves to be depraved, and partly because experience shows us much goodness in human nature." [67] But the doctrine, in fact, does not deny that there is some goodness in human nature; it basically argues that man's will is in bondage and every virtue is tainted by pride. Ironically, in other places Lewis does reject the heart of the doctrine (without apparently knowing it), when he denies that man's will is in bondage and that he is unable to turn to God. Paradisal Man, in Lewis' view, could still turn back to God, though only by painful effort because his natural inclination was selfward. Here is an example of Lewis' occasional insufficient grasp of the finer points of theology.

Salvation

All men are in principle saved in the vicarious death of Christ, but salvation must be appropriated by individuals. Salvation involves the universal principle of dying to live. But man in himself cannot follow the path of perfect penitence. Salvation does not involve doing something so much as abandoning all efforts of self-preservation. It is submission to the grace of God in which man receives *zoe* as well as *bios*, spiritual as well as biological life. Christ is the "carrier" of new life, and man must get close enough to catch the infection from him. It is a process in which God creates new men and we come to share in the life of Christ. Salvation begins as a decision and continues as a process of perfecting in life and even beyond the grave, as imperfection is purged and we are made like Christ.

Lewis' most striking picture of transformation into a new man is in *The Voyage of the Dawn Treader* where Eustace is changed from a dragon back into a boy. Eustace, a despicably spoiled brat, had been turned into a dragon while sleeping in a dragon's cave which he entered because of greed. Aslan the lion (a mythological figure for Christ), desiring to turn him back into a boy, led him to a pool of water and instructed him to undress. After peeling off three successive layers of dragon skin only to find himself each time exactly as before, Eustace in desperation lay down and let Aslan rip off his skin (it seemed to him, right down to his heart). When finished, Aslan threw the soft and peeled Eustace into the water, took him out, and dressed him in new clothes. The result was a new Eustace, transformed by the power of Aslan.

The story of Eustace illustrates Lewis' belief that if you give God an inch, he will take a mile. The Christian believer sometimes gets more than he bargained for, because God's goal in salvation is perfection. But in submitting to God's radical surgery, man gets everything in return. By giving himself to God, he receives back his true self. By giving God his highest love, he finds that all lesser loves take on new value. By seeking the new life in God and nothing else, he discovers that the old life takes on new meaning. Far from taking a man out of the world, salvation returns a man to the world to continue doing most of the same old things in a new spirit, sanctifying the common tasks of life. Whatever the Christian does, he does all to the glory of God.

Lewis tries to maintain the paradox of salvation between God's activity and man's response. It is as we begin to dress up like Christ and God is beginning to turn our pretense into reality that we become aware both of our sinfulness and of God doing everything for us. The church exists to draw men into Christ, and it is within the Christian communion that the saving presence of God is most known. But this is not to say that those outside the church cannot be saved. No one is saved outside of Christ, but this does not necessarily involve a knowledge of Christ. Some are more deeply attached to Christ than they understand. Men outside of the Christian revelation, and perhaps some who know the revelation in a confused way, may be saved by concentrating on the elements in their religion that are most compatible with Christianity.[68]

The Church and the Sacraments

Though not speaking in detail or clearly about the church, Lewis accepts the Anglican idea of the church as an extension of the incarnation. The mass of Christians are the physical organism, the body of Christ, through which Christ continues to act. Quite literally, Christians are Christ's body, his fingers and muscles and cells. Every new member of the body helps him to do more in the world.

The church as an organized institution — the sales work, parish magazine, bell ringing — was relatively unimportant to Lewis. Those kinds of "religious" activities are no more important than many so-called secular activities, and they may, in reality, distract one from genuinely Christian actions. But the church as a spiritual fellowship was of great importance to him because it helps to nourish the spiritual life and spread Christ in the world. The church, as the mystical body of Christ, stands in contrast to all secular collectivism or individualism. Christians are members or organs of the body, " things essentially different from, and complementary to, one another: things differing not only in structure and function but also in dignity."⁶⁹ Within the organic union, where men worship, sacrifice the self daily, and love and show Christ to one another, true personality growth occurs and self-identity is achieved. The church is the only adequate instrument for learning about God and spreading the Christian infection.

Lewis in a sense views the church as the mediator of salvation. In *The Pilgrim's Regress*, it is Mother Kirk who must lead John and Vertue across the Grand Canyon which separates them from the Landlord's country. And yet, salvation occurs outside the visible church, *through* Christ but without *knowing* about Christ. Some pagans reach the church. "That is the definition," says Lewis, "of a Pagan — a man so travelling that if all goes well he arrives at Mother Kirk's chair and is carried over this gorge." ⁷⁰ But the best way to help those outside the knowledge of Christ is to be joined to the church oneself.

The body of Christ analogy helps Lewis to understand how the Christian life is spread through bodily acts such as Baptism and Communion as well as mental acts such as belief. Though not understanding how these become conductors of the new life, he accepts all three on authority. Because the Sacraments have been so divisive in the church, Lewis said little about them. He recognized that people in different communions would want to emphasize one or another above the others.

However, in his last Christian work, *Letters to Malcolm*, he did discuss Holy Communion. His belief in the "real" presence of Christ is uniquely stamped with his view of transposition and the continuity between the physical and spiritual. Physical bread and wine are transposed into vehicles that carry spiritual life. Finding the Catholic view and the symbolic view equally unsatisfactory, he dares to call his own view "magical," which he defines as "objective efficacy which cannot be further analysed." ⁷¹ Although not rationally understanding how the elements are Christ's body and blood or how partaking of Communion relates to incorporation in the Christian community, he thinks that the veil between the worlds is nowhere else both so opaque to the intellect and so thin and permeable to the divine operation. "Here is big medicine and strong magic." [72] The important thing, however, is to take and eat, not to take and understand.

The Christian Life

Lewis' view of ethics is a conglomeration of Biblical literalism, philosophical ethics, broad principles, legalistic rules, penetrating psychological insights, and strange silences. Ethics occupies much of *The Case for Christianity* and *Christian Behaviour*, and finds expression in *The Screwtape Letters*, *The Pilgrim's Regress*, and *The Great Divorce*. Lewis' ethical views are like a kaleidoscope: turn a page and you are not always sure what you will find. At times legalistic, he is never puritanical. For example, the Christian rule about sex is either unmitigated monogamy or complete abstinence. But he does not disparage sex, for within marriage, sex involves pleasure and play, fierceness and laughter. Or again, he presents a paradoxical view about murder. He condemns hatred as murder and was an active antivivisectionist, yet refuses to reject capital punishment or war. He severely criticizes sins of the spirit, yet exhibits compassionate understanding of sins of the flesh. "A cold, self-righteous prig who goes regularly to church," he suggests, "may be far nearer to hell than a prostitute. But, of course, it is far better to be neither." [73] His economic views are rather advanced and "socialistic," while his code for family life and personal manners is rather "old-fashioned" by modern standards.

One thing is certain. Lewis would have no part of our contemporary "new morality." He wrote, "There never has been, and never will be, a radically new judgment of value in the history of the world." [74] New moralities are simply elements of Natural Law that are wrenched from their context and swollen to madness in their isolation. There can be progress in insights within the framework of Natural Law, which is the sole source of all value judgments, but only quacks and cranks introduce new moralities. Even Christ did not teach a radical new morality. The Golden Rule is only a summing up of what people had always known to be right. The cardinal virtues of prudence, temperance, justice, and fortitude are recognized by all civilized people. Moral rules are rules for running the human machine, or descriptions of how man is intended to function. They are expressions in terms of temporal existence of what God by his own righteous nature necessarily is. For that reason Lewis could never think of God or the Christian life as "beyond morality." God may be more than moral; he is not less nor other than moral. "The road to the promised land runs past Sinai." [75]

Distinctive Christian morality begins only with the theological virtues of faith, hope, and love, which meet the three concerns of morality: harmony within the individual, relations between individuals, and the general purpose of life. The Christian life involves both faith in Christ and good actions. By faith the sinner is changed into a new man, making Christian moral actions possible by God working in him. Love then governs his relations with men, and hope provides the purpose of life. Lewis' brand of Christianity is not escapist or otherworldly. Only heaven satisfies the human longing, but aiming at it infuses life and the world with meaning and value.

A key principle for Lewis is that growth and progress are more important in ethical action than relative achievement. The Christian demand is so stringent, and yet the Christian tolerance of failure is so great. That paradox is because the goal of the Christian is perfection, but Christians are found at all stages of growth, facing varied handicaps that make choices easy or difficult. There are two elements in the moral person: (1) the essential, choosing self, and (2) the raw materials — the physiology, the psychological makeup, the family and social relations — out of which moral choices are made. The individual is not always responsible for his own raw materials, but the raw materials of the personality limit moral choices.

Therefore, niceness, pleasantness, and a wholesome personality do not always indicate spiritual health or achievement; they may be only a congenital gift from God. Man judges on the basis of actions alone. God sees beneath the level of raw materials to the depth of intention in the choosing self, and judges man on a more profound basis. God is more concerned with man's intention and the way he is headed than with his relative stage of accomplishment. God is easy to please but hard to satisfy. He is pleased with the first stumbling steps of Christian living; he is satisfied only by perfection. The demand for perfection, combined with his realistic view of man's imperfection, almost forces Lewis to the idea of purgatory, as we shall see. The man of faith will be perfected, either in life or beyond the grave. The goal of Christian living is always ahead. Onward and upward, farther up and farther in — that is the battle cry of the Christian.

A cornerstone of Lewis' approach to life is the goodness of creation. Lewis was once accused of being a Manichee — which is preposterous. He is as far from that as possible. He affirms the goodness of matter, the body, the senses, all pleasures, and all values — of art, music, culture, and human institutions. All created things are intrinsically good and, if properly used, can be used and done to the glory of God. Lewis admits a proper place for Christian renunciation, but not for asceticism. Christian renunciation, however, is not stoic apathy, but is the preference of God over inferior ends.

Because of the Fall, there is a present quarrel between the body and the spirit. But by this Lewis means that the spirit sends desires down to the body, not that the body sends desires up to the mind. He says: " Bless the body. Mine has led me into many scrapes, but I've led it into far more. If the imagination were obedient the appetites would give us very little trouble. And from how much it has saved me! " [76] That is far from Manicheeism. Rather than disparage the body, he affirms its sanctity and value.

He approaches sex in the same spirit. Sex is morally neutral.

Its goodness or badness depends on how it is used. Sexual pleasure is proper within a monogamous union of love; it becomes a monstrosity outside of marriage or when it becomes an end in itself within marriage, because it isolates sexual union from the total union. Sex within marriage should be neither solemnized or disparaged. Through nudity a man and his wife participate in universal masculinity and femininity, the pagan sacrament in sex. There is a good roughness and fierceness, comedy and play, even buffoonery in sex; it is both a grandeur and a joke, with the lovers always laughing at each other. Lewis considers Christianity to be the only great religion that thoroughly approves of the body and glorifies marriage. Sensuality is the perversion of legitimate pleasures, so that pleasures grow smaller while cravings grow larger.

Screwtape warns Wormwood that God is a Hedonist, and that all pleasures come from him. And Lewis found a wide assortment of pleasures — of love, friendship, solitude, sex, study, culture, walking, eating, and drinking. The sensuous beauty of nature finds expression in all of Lewis' writings. He loved the wetness of the rain, the heat of the sun, the mountains and the sea, the beauty of ugliness, " the very quiddity of each thing." The appetites of man for knowledge, beauty, culture, and nature are not made in vain, and, when properly used, help advance man toward the vision of God. As Screwtape says: "He has filled His world full of pleasures. There are things for humans to do all day long without His minding in the least — sleeping, washing, eating, drinking, making love, playing, praying, working. Everything has to be *twisted* before it's any use to us." [77] Literally, a "smell of Deity" hangs over life. Pleasures, either sensuous or aesthetic, are "shafts of the glory as it strikes our sensibility." [78] In revealing God to the Christian, they provide occasion for "adoration in infinitesimals." Pleasures become bad only when they are used in the wrong way or directed to the wrong end.

Lewis, with some justification, has been castigated for ignoring the social implications of the Christian faith. But fairness demands that one understand his reasons. For one thing, the Christian faith contains no detailed program that is applicable to a particular society at a particular moment. For another, Lewis felt no special competence in applying Christianity to social problems. Further, he felt that social Christianity always risks the temptation to make Christianity only a means to some other end, to make it the support for a certain economic or political program, some social reform, or some other compulsive interest. Screwtape even suggests that by tempting man to use Christianity as a means to such a noble end as social justice, he can be made to use God as a convenience. Some current fashion with a Christian coloring can take the place of faith itself. Social Christianity also runs the danger of attempting to legislate Christian morality, for example, on marriage or drinking liquor. Instead, the Christian must frankly recognize that he lives in a secular society and that the church ought to regulate itself and not the broader culture.

Despite reservations, he did not completely ignore social problems. But he approached collective problems on an individual basis, believing that Christians ought to act like Christians in their various vocations. What advocates of social Christianity usually mean is that the Christian clergy ought to provide programs for economics, politics, labor relations, and international relations. But that is asking them to do a job for which they are not trained. The solution is for Christians in specialized vocations to apply Christian principles to social problems — in trade unions, education, or politics, just as Christian novelists and dramatists produce Christian literature. The basic social principle is active beneficence. Beyond that the Christian faith does not speak directly. Lewis plainly states: "Of forms of government, of civil authority and civil obedience, I have nothing to say." [79]

Obviously, this "hands off" attitude leaves him out of step with current social Christianity. Here is one of Lewis' weakest points. And yet in his silence he has something to say to a large segment of the contemporary church. To Christians who are increasingly becoming preoccupied with "Coffeehouse Christianity," and who are more interested in expressing human concern than in redeeming people; to zealous clergymen who deem themselves authorities in economics, labor-management relations, international policies, and other problems, Lewis serves a warning. If the "social" Christian replies that he is attempting to find new ways to make the Christian faith relevant, Lewis could claim that as his lifelong preoccupation, but with a difference. He spoke in pubs on the waterfront, to soldiers and airmen, to college students, to the common man on the B.B.C. He used common language in unusual literary forms, but it was always with the intention to confront people with the necessity and urgency of decision; to express love and concern, but also to introduce men to the God of Love. Currently, much of the church has fallen into the very kinds of preoccupation that alarmed Lewis. The social gospel contains truth that Lewis failed to grasp. But Lewis advocated truths that some proponents of social Christianity have forgotten: the importance of personal as well as social morality, the seriousness of individual as well as collective sin, the necessity of redeeming individuals as well as social institutions, the value of being a "member" of the church as well as being a Christian in the world. Since the church is always only one generation from extinction, there is hellish wisdom in Screwtape's advice about becoming "Christians with a difference." Now our theme is "Christianity and Social Concern." The danger is that in its preoccupation with expressing human concern rather than converting men, the church might die a quiet death, as death systematically eliminates its "concerned" members who have reached no new converts to take their place. And those who benefited from Christian "concern" may have received a cup of coffee, or a welfare check, or better education, or decent housing — and lost their souls. What Lewis should have known is that housing, education, welfare, and economics are important. What Lewis has to say is that they must not become ends in themselves.

Eschatology

Eschatology plays a dominant role in Lewis' thinking and writing. Nowhere is his approach to the mythopoeic nature of language more clearly seen. Here he does in practice what he advocates in principle: take the Biblical symbols seriously without taking them literally. He believes in devils, angels, purgatory, heaven and hell, the second coming, the resurrection of the body, and the judgment. These eschatological ideas pervade his writings and underline the eternal finality with which he views temporal choices. Eschatological concern motivates his apologetic efforts. Each individual, by his small daily choices, is at every moment living under the shadow of eternal issues and advancing to either heaven or hell. Man is involved in the universal conflict between good and evil.

Devils and Angels. The devil provides part of Lewis' explanation for the evil in the world. Although it is not essential to his religion or part of his creed, he believes in angels and demons because the Scripture, church tradition, and most men have believed in them, and the belief does not conflict with modern science. But he does not think of them as pictured in art and literature, although admittedly any higher beings in the natural world would necessarily have to be represented symbolically. Talk of angels and devils and hell, while referring to concrete reality, is indispensable myth and symbol that help to explain evil in the universe and our sense of involvement in the conflict between good and evil.

The devil is not eternally self-existent. God has no "perfect badness" as an eternal opposite; the devil cannot succeed in being bad as God is perfectly good. Evil is a parasite; it is derivative. To be bad, evil must exist and have intelligence and will, which are good things that only God can give. Lewis believes in devils because he believes in angels. Speaking mythologically, he accepts the traditional view that God created angels and that some of them, by the abuse of free will, became enemies of God and occupied the world. The devil, who represents these fallen angels, is the power behind death, disease, and sin. Man lives in rebel-occupied territory. That theme is vividly brought out in Lewis' space triology, where the earth is the " silent planet" that has been isolated by God because of the fallen angel who rules it. God has invaded this enemy-occupied territory once in disguise; one day he will return in force. Until then, the devils are engaged in attempting to subvert and devour men and defeat God.

Hell. Lewis' *The Great Divorce* is his imaginative attempt to portray the divorce between heaven and hell and the absolutely unavoidable either-or of life. Each man is faced with innumerable choices, and each choice represents a step on the road toward the perfection of good or evil of which heaven or hell will be the culmination. One's future state is only a mimicry of choices made on earth — which is the beginning of heaven or hell — and is an eternal attainment of his earthly wishes. Heaven and hell are the logical outcome of God's respect for human freedom. George Macdonald tells Lewis: " There are only two kinds of people in the end: those who say to God, ' Thy will be done,' and those to whom God says, in the end, '*Thy* will be done.' All that are in Hell, choose it. Without that self-choice there could be no Hell." [80]

Lewis' belief in hell is based on the authority of the Scripture, the church, and reason. Hell is necessitated by two factors: the justice of God and the freedom of man. Justice demands retributive punishment for those who continue to sin without remorse or repentance, so that the flag of right may be planted in the rebellious soul to mercifully cure him of his self-illusion. Judgment, as well as being retributive, consists in God abandoning men to their own desires. Hell means the defeat of divine omnipotence, but that is the great gamble God takes when he refuses to override man's free will. Thus the damned are successful rebels to the end, and, in that sense, the doors of hell are locked on the inside by the human will. Their wills are so fixed inward that a second chance after death would be of no avail. Their motto is: " Better to reign in Hell than serve in Heaven." [81] At the same time, no soul that seriously and constantly desires heaven will miss it.

Lewis takes the images for hell seriously but not literally. The three scriptural images of hell — as punishment, destruction, and privation or exclusion — converge in the idea of being banished from humanity and going to a place never meant for men at all. To enter heaven is for the first time to become fully man, with the passions obedient to the will and the will obedient to God. What is banished to hell is only the " remains " of a man that has uncontrolled passions and an utterly self-centered will. In hell the " ghosts " of men enjoy and are enslaved by the horrible freedom they have willed.

The terrors of hell pictured in the Scripture emphasize the idea not of duration but of finality. Whether hell has duration is impossible to say, but it must not be treated as a parallel to heaven. It is the darkness outside. A constant theme of Lewis is that hell " is so nearly Nothing." In fact, the redeemed are not small enough to get into hell. " Nothing like small enough," he writes. " For a damned soul is nearly nothing: it is shrunk, shut up in itself." [82] The damned soul is the outworking of earthly decisions in which the sinner becomes his sin. The grumbler is reduced to a Grumble, the flirtatious female to Flirtation, the ambitious wife to Ambition, the sensual man to Sensuality. Their humanity is so reduced that no longer are they capable of either criticizing or enjoying their sins. They have become, as Lewis described them, " grotesque phantoms in which hardly a trace of the human form remained." [83] Weston, the scientist in the first two space novels, so perfectly becomes Evil Incarnate that Lewis calls him the " Un-man."

This view of the " nothingness " of hell overcomes some of the chief objections about the doctrine. Joy in heaven can in no way be diminished by souls in a hell that is so nearly nothing and is no parallel to heaven. Hell must not in this way be allowed to veto heaven. Lewis thinks a tension must be maintained between predestination and universal salvation. Emotionally he would like to eliminate the doctrine of hell, but honesty compels him to retain it. He would like for all men to be saved, but his reason asks, "Without their will, or with it?" Of those who object to the doctrine, he asks: "'What are you asking God to do?' To wipe out their past sins and, at all costs, to give them a fresh start, smoothing every difficulty and offering every miraculous help? But He has done so, on Calvary. To forgive them? They will not be forgiven. To leave them alone? Alas, I am afraid that is what He does." [84]

Heaven. To critics who suggest that heaven plays too prominent a role in his thinking, Lewis could reply that he believed in God before he believed in heaven. Aside from that, heaven and hell either exist or do not exist; if they do, they must occupy an important place in Christian thinking. Heaven is important only because God is there, but his presence makes heaven the true home of man and the source of man's longing and sense of estrangement in the world. Man's immortal longings, a "weight of glory" that he bears, contain tantalizing glimpses of heaven.[85] Heaven is the world of solid, concrete reality of which the earth is only a shadow. It is as different from the world as a real thing is from a shadow or as waking life from a dream. Digory speaks for Lewis in saying, "It's all in Plato, all in Plato: bless me, what do they teach them at these schools!" [86] The same idea is drawn in *The Great Divorce* where the heavenly terrain is too solid for any but the Solid People who have been perfected by God.

We gain glimpses of heaven in the high moments of human experience, creating a longing which is frequently attached to false objects or called by names like Nostalgia and Romanticism and Adolescence. All the experiences bear witness that our real goal is elsewhere. Lewis called the experience *Sehnsucht*, as we have seen. *Sehnsucht* was the driving force of his life before he became a Christian. A part of his experience, he made it an important part of his apologetic, as we will later examine. But the longing for heaven pervades his writings, and at times his vision of heaven, apocalyptic in scope, becomes poignantly, even painfully, beautiful. The longing for heaven is a worthy motive in the Christian life, because love always seeks to enjoy its object. Proper rewards are the activity itself in consummation. Just as marriage is a proper reward of the true lover, heaven is the proper reward of the Christian.

Lewis is clear that the images and symbols of heaven — the harps, crowns, gold, music, and so on — are attempts to express the inexpressible, and obviously are not to be taken literally. The attempt to dispense with the Biblical images finds us smuggling in the ideas of proximity in space and loving conversation, or perhaps hymeneal or erotic imagery. The promises of Scripture are roughly five: that we shall be with Christ, be like Christ, have " glory," be feasted and entertained, and have some official ruling position in the universe. The promises do not mean that anything other than God will be our bliss, but they help enlarge our present poor experience of love. A dozen changing images are provided to correct and relieve each other.

But the Scriptural images have divine authority, and are more than we can surmise ourselves. The idea of glory, when carefully examined, is pregnant with distinctive meaning that fills out our idea of heaven. Glory satisfies our original desire and reveals an element often overlooked — the desire to be participants, not merely spectators, in the real world. " For glory," writes Lewis, " means good report with God, acceptance by God, response, acknowledgement, and welcome into the heart of things." In this sense, glory means fame with God, the divine accolade, approval by God. But glory also conveys the idea of brightness, splendor, luminosity. This sense of glory represents the overlooked element of our desire: the desire not only to see beauty, but " to be united with the beauty we see, to pass into it, to receive it into ourselves, to bathe in it, to become part of it." [87] At that point, passing beyond nature, the saved soul will flow over into the glorified body.

Purgatory. Before heaven and the glorified state, there is purgatory. Belief in purgatory is the outcome of Lewis' view of the necessary perfecting of the individual. Our souls, in his view, demand purgatory. Before entering the presence of God, we would beg to be taken and cleansed. Purgatory, then, is a place of purification and perfecting, not torment. That purification may involve suffering, just as pulling a tooth involves pain, but God will be there to rinse out the wounds. Lewis therefore prayed for the dead, believing that prayers are eternally known to God and are taken into account in his dealings with the blessed dead. How consistent Lewis' view of purgatory is with the New Testament teachings about justification, forgiveness, and reconciliation would be debated by Christians in different communions. But in his personal devotional life, it had great impact. To God's invitation, " Enter into joy," he would reply, " If there is no objection, I'd *rather* be clean first." [88] He thought of his deceased wife in purgatory as " a splendid thing; a soul straight, bright, and tempered like a sword. But not a perfected saint. A sinful woman married to a sinful man; two of God's patients, not yet cured. I know there are not only tears to be dried but stains to be scoured. The sword will be made even brighter.

" But oh God, tenderly, tenderly." [89]

The Resurrection of the Body. Lewis conjectures that the blessed dead may exist in naked spirituality in purgatory. But the heavenly life will require the resurrection of the body. Here again he retains the image and interprets its meaning. He makes a most interesting conjecture that the resurrection of the body means the resurrection of the sensuous life, which is another instance of transposition, as the beatific experience of God floods and transvalues the senses, creating an appropriate correspondence on the sensory level to the beatific vision. Heaven becomes a transsensuous existence. This doctrine is not concerned with matter as such. The heavenly body is not the physical body restored. Rather, we cry out for resurrection of the senses. He speculates that the glorified body will be within soul, as space is within God and not God in space. By being perceived and known through sensation and conception, matter enters into our experience and is turned into soul. And that element in soul which matter becomes is what will be raised and glorified. The hills and valleys of heaven will relate to those of earth as a flower to the root or a diamond to coal. The glorified body of the sensuous life and the material world will be within the perceiving and knowing soul. The blessed dead will return and again take up their bodies. "Then the new earth and sky, the same yet not the same as these, will rise in us as we have risen in Christ. And once again, after who knows what aeons of the silence and the dark, the birds will sing out and the waters flow, and lights and shadows move across the hills and the faces of our friends laugh upon us with amazed recognition.

"Guesses, of course, only guesses. If they are not true, something better will be. For we know that we shall be made like Him, for we shall see Him as He is." [90]

The Second Coming. The fact of the second coming gives life's daily decisions apocalyptic significance. The doctrine conflicts with modern evolutionary thought that Lewis regards as a myth, an attempt to guess the plot of the world drama. The doctrine of the Second Coming teaches us that we cannot know when the drama will end and the curtain be rung down. It is precisely the medicine the modern world needs. Cutting through the apocalyptic imagery, Lewis considers Christ's teachings on his return to consist of three propositions: "(1) That he will certainly return. (2) That we cannot possibly find out when. (3) And that therefore we must always be ready for him." [91] The doctrine should not be used to create fear or crisis-feeling or idle speculation. But it should always be taken into account, as though this present may be the world's last night. What should be kept in mind is not the picture of physical catastrophe, but the naked idea of judgment, of an infallibly perfect verdict that will be passed on us all. Since we do not know when Christ will return, today is the time to choose the right side.

His theology, like his apologetic, converges at the point of decision. Man walks daily on the razor's edge between the incredible possibilities of damnation or salvation. He should ask himself, "What if this present were the world's last night?" [92]

Communication: The Mastery of a Difficult Art

During the twentieth century, England has produced a remarkable group of popular interpreters of the Christian faith — among them, G. K. Chesterton, Dorothy Sayers, J. B. Phillips, and, especially, C. S. Lewis. They have shared an uncommon ability to communicate simply and clearly, with the result that their writings have been widely read.

Whatever the merits of Lewis' thought or view of the Christian faith, even his bitterest critics admit that his ideas are presented with style, dash, and brilliance. A reviewer of his *English Literature in the Sixteenth Century Excluding Drama* called him "the virtuoso of literary history; he is like a violinist who makes up his own cadenzas." [93] His writing has been called a model of contemporary English. He has a bag full of literary tricks from which he adroitly pulls metaphor, analogy, allegory, illustration, epigram, epithet, bravura, and hyperbole to fit his purpose. His use of metaphor alone is a major study. The startling metaphor, the felicitous phrase, the soaring of imagination provide a fertile loam for the flowering of his ideas. His gracefulness of style is enhanced by his dry wit, his sharp satire, and his use of irony, ridicule, and sarcasm.

The most striking feature of his writing is the conversational style. What one would expect to be confined to the *Broadcast Talks* is a characteristic of all his writing (with the exception of perhaps *The Pilgrim's Regress* and *Till We Have Faces*). Even scholarly works like *English Literature in the Sixteenth Century Excluding Drama*, *The Discarded Image*, or *The Allegory of Love* retain a personal conversational style — more formally, to be sure, but it is still there. The reader never feels lectured at or detached from the author. Rather, one feels that he and C. S. Lewis are sitting down over tea to discuss an intensely interesting subject — whatever it might be. The scholarly works are never stodgily or stuffily academic, and the Christian writings are never pious moralizings; the twinkling eye and good humor of Lewis prevent that. Nor does one feel that he has entered an esoteric world. There is no consciousness of "big" words or of any specialized theological or literary critical jargon. Any reasonably well educated person can intelligently read all of Lewis' writings. Lewis overcomes the almost insurmountable obstacle of encasing his ideas in brilliant trappings and yet making the reader more aware of his ideas than his style.

It is universally conceded that his mastery of the art of communication was the principal reason for his popularity. The appeal of his apologetic writings is in their artistic quality as well as in the knowledge they communicate — a rare accomplishment for an apologist. As a writer, Lewis stands with his feet in two often contrasting fields. Literature in its widest sense includes both the literature of knowledge (scientific and informative writings) and the literature of power (artistic writings). Most traditional apologetic writings fall strictly into the category of the literature of knowledge. But Lewis' writings in a unique fashion bridge the gap between the literature of knowledge and the literature of power; they rise from the dry dust of logic into the invigorating atmosphere of art. Professional apologists and theologians, if they want to learn from Lewis' mastery of the apologetic craft, would be well advised to examine carefully his writing style and his ideas on communication. That study should include not only his distinctive apologetic writings but also his works in literary criticism. From the standpoint of what constitutes good writing, works like *The Personal Heresy, The Allegory of Love, Studies in Words, An Experiment in Criticism,* and various essays are invaluable.

Although Lewis' literary theory was formed primarily in relation to the literature of power (or art), much of it can be usefully applied to any writing, to argumentative as well as to strictly artistic writings, to apologetic literature as well as to literature in general. The works on literary criticism are of value to the apologist partly because of Lewis' view that there are no qualities peculiar to Christian literature. The rules for writing Christian literature — whether a passion play, a devotional lyric, or a discursive book — are the same as those for tragic, lyric, or discursive literature in general. Lewis writes: "Boiling an egg is the same process whether you are a Christian or a Pagan. . . . [Whatever Christian literature chooses] to do would have to be done by the means common to all literature; it could succeed or fail only by the same excellences and the same faults as all literature." [94] Our present interest is not to discuss thoroughly his literary theory, but to extract from his theory certain key principles that can be related to the art of communicating the Christian faith.

As a critic, Lewis was sensitive to the rapidly changing standards of literary criticism, enough so that he could usually date with some accuracy the age of people by what authors they like. He believed that critical standards must transcend the passing phases of contemporary judgments. Lewis was remarkably catholic in his own literary tastes and had a fondness for some books that current critics consider poor writing. Therefore, Lewis proposed that the standards of criticism be reversed. He established as a critical principle that good books invite good reading, by which he means the surrendering of oneself to the work that one is reading and entering fully into the opinions of others. A good book facilitates self-transcendence. As Lewis says, " In reading great literature I become a thousand men and yet remain myself. . . . Here, as in worship, in love, in moral action, and in knowing, I transcend myself, and am never more myself than when I do." [95] Thus Lewis held, and thinks Christians should hold, an almost hedonistic view of the literature of power, so that literature should be valued not for telling us truths about life, or as an aid to culture, but as an end in itself. Literature is an art that is to be enjoyed. It is paradoxical that because Lewis' own writings interweave so closely his art with what he says about life, his hedonistic standard of judgment cannot be rigorously applied to his own writings, even the books of fiction.

But Lewis underlines what, unhappily, too many apologists have forgotten: that an apologetic effort is literature as well as argument. What Lewis says about the character of literary art can be applied to apologetic writings. Literary art, he writes, " both *means* and *is*. It is both *Logos* (something said) and *Poiema* (something made). As Logos it tells a story, or expresses an emotion, or exhorts or pleads or describes or rebukes or excites laughter. As Poiema, by its aural beauties and also by the balance and contrast and the unified multiplicity of its successive parts, it is an *objet d'art*, a thing shaped so as to give great satisfaction." [96] Both the Logos and the Poiema are important. " It is only by being a Poiema that a Logos becomes a work of literary art at all." [97] But conversely, " it is out of our various interests in the Logos that the Poiema is made." [98] Good books allow a man to enlarge his being.

Lewis, in *The Personal Heresy*, laid down two criteria for literature of value to which he tenaciously held. The first demand of any writing is that it be interesting. Lewis considered the greatest sin in literature to be dullness and the greatest purpose of literature to produce enjoyment. His deep feeling on that is underscored in *That Hideous Strength* where Lewis portrays Dr. Dimble's reluctance in excusing himself from tea: " ' There is my dullest pupil just ringing the bell,' he said. ' I must go to the study, and listen to an essay on Swift beginning, " Swift was born." Must try to keep my mind on it too, which won't be easy.' " [99] Lewis allows that the literature may be interesting for all sorts of reasons, since different things interest different people; but it must be interesting.

The second demand of any writing of value is that it " should have a desirable permanent effect on us if possible — should make us either happier, or wiser, or better." [100] There is nothing " moral " in this demand. It is merely a question of " whether this enjoyment wears well and helps or hinders you toward all the other things you would like to enjoy, to do, or be." [101]

From these principles, it emerges that good apologetic writing should be interesting and have a permanent effect on the reader. To do so, apologetic writing should help the reader to stand in the apologist's shoes and see with his eyes, imagine with his imagination, reason with his reason, and feel with his heart, to break out of his own monad and get into the monad of another, which can be described as an enlargement or a temporary annihilation of the self.

Adapting those simple criteria for literary value, Lewis rejects the contemporary exclusive emphasis on spontaneity, creativity, originality, and self-expression in literature. His view has much more in common with the Homeric theory of the poet as " the mere pensioner of the Muse " and the Platonic theory of transcendent Forms partly imitable on earth. The Christian writer may be self-taught and original, or he may use established forms and ideas common to the race. Either way makes no difference. The important thing is to respond to the " vision " as his individual talent dictates. " And always, of every idea and of every method he will ask not ' Is it mine?,' but ' Is it good? ' "[102] Consistent with that view, Lewis selected his own literary forms to fit his purpose. He did not hesitate to pattern *The Pilgrim's Regress* after Bunyan's *The Pilgrim's Progress*, and Dante's *Divine Comedy* influenced the dream-journey form of *The Great Divorce*. His space trilogy and children's novels use established forms. Yet there is sparkling originality in *The Screwtape Letters* and *Letters to Malcolm*. Ostensibly, of every idea and every method Lewis asked not " It it mine? " but " Is it good? " In the same way, every Christian writer should work to master literary style.

The second element in the art of communication is the mastery of words. Lewis was enchanted by the power and beauty of words. It is not accidental that his space hero, Ransom, is a philologist. Lewis' lifelong interest in the origin, etymology, and meaning of words, and his method of comparative study, is clearly seen in his *Studies in Words*.

Language poses at least three practical problems for the Christian apologist. First, language, with its limitations, must communicate the highest reality. The apologist's problem is how to make the ultimate understandable in historical terms. His only vehicle is language. A recurrent theme in Lewis is that reality is too definite, not indefinite, for language. Therefore, the apologist must come to understand the nature of language, its relation to reality, and become adept at using it to talk about ultimate reality.

The second problem is that language is a living, changing thing; it is never static and words both take on new meaning through ramification and also lose their vitality through verbicide. We have already examined Lewis' contention that originally a close correspondence existed between language and reality. But language is never static and words constantly take on new meaning, much as a tree throws out branches that in turn throw out other branches — a process of ramification. A study of words is essential to anyone who communicates. Lewis admits: "Prolonged thought *about* the words which we ordinarily use to think *with* can produce a momentary aphasia. I think it is to be welcomed. It is well we should become aware of what we are doing when we speak, of the ancient, fragile, and (well used) immensely potent instruments that words are." [103]

Verbicide is continually committed in the process of change, the most important way being by altering descriptive into evaluative words so that sharp, good words fall into a eulogistic or dyslogistic abyss and become mere synonyms for good and bad. Words like " Christian," " civilized," " gentleman," or " contemporary " lose their distinctive meanings and are simply used eulogistically; words like " adolescent," " derivative," or " vulgar " are used dyslogistically.

Because of the processes of ramification and verbicide, the particular meaning of a word is not always self-evident. The word itself usually has different senses that are defined and limited by its literary context and historical era. Further, the word itself may have a different meaning than as used by the writer or understood by the reader. Sometimes the writer will not use the word as he defines it, in which case it is better to see how he uses it than how he defines it. So the apologist must become sensitive to the evolution of language.

THE FOUNDATION OF APOLOGETICS 137

The third problem is that, in contemporary society, language has different meanings for different classes of people, which requires both the empirical study of how they use words and a continual translation of theological jargon into the vernacular. Lewis considered this problem to be particularly acute in England where there are almost two languages, the learned and the vulgar. In speaking with the common man, it is not enough to refrain from using difficult words. The apologist must discover empirically what words exist in the vocabulary of his audience and what they mean in their language. In various places, Lewis cites numerous examples of words as used by ordinary Englishmen — of how, for example, potential means not "possible" but "power," primitive means "rude" or "clumsy," the Immaculate Conception means the "virgin birth," morality means "chastity," practical means "economic" or "utilitarian," and Christian is a eulogistic synonym for "good."

Having discovered how his audience uses words, the apologist must engage in the process of adapting complex ideas to the language and word meanings of his audience, of translating theological and philosophic jargon into the vernacular. Therefore, Lewis states a fundamental principle for all who would communicate the Christian faith: "Any fool can write *learned* language. The vernacular is the real test. If you can't turn your faith into it, then either you don't understand it or you don't believe it." [104] Lewis believed the ability to translate technical theology to be so important that he argued every ordination examination should require the translation of a passage from a standard theological work into the vernacular, which could expose either ignorance of the vernacular or ignorance of the theological meaning. "It is absolutely disgraceful," he suggests, "that we expect missionaries to the Bantus to learn Bantu but never ask whether our missionaries to the Americans or English can speak American or English." [105]

The attempt to translate the Christian faith into the language of the common man, which permeates his writings, is most clearly seen in the *Broadcast Talks*. Of that attempt, Alistair Cooke, an archcritic of Lewis, wrote that unlike most professional men in radio he was not " merely wiring his normal writing style for sound. He knows that radio should find an idiom, and images, that will mean the same thing to people of very different background, an ambition that only our gag-writers seem to sweat over. He knows it is the first task of radio to make ideas honestly clear. . . . He has to explain the Beatitudes in words of one syllable." [106] Cooke concludes that Lewis fails in a pseudo simplicity. But that is the task he set for himself in all his writings — to communicate simply and understandably to the masses of people.

Some critics evidently do not agree with his intention. Lewis' brilliant use of the vernacular resulted in the accusation that he was " playing to the gallery " and using cleverness in place of rational argument. He was accused of crudity, vulgarity, and irreverence because of the words, expressions, and ideas he used. But Lewis' semantic usage and argumentative structures were usually carefully selected in line with his attempt to cast his apologetic into the vernacular.

Let us consider an obvious example. His famous Christological alternative, where Lewis poses the choice between Christ as the " Son of God," a " raving lunatic of an unusually abominable type," or a " devil," is a perfect example of using language that communicates. " Lunatic " is repellent to the well-educated, sensitive person who would prefer to say that Jesus may have been a " megalomaniac " or had " delusions of grandeur." The average man, however, knows little of megalomania or delusions of grandeur, but he does know that lunatic means " insane " or " mad." George E. Lee's objection that this is not the Christian approach to lunatics misses the point.[107] Lewis is using a word that has meaning to a mass audience; it has a crisp, cutting edge and needs no further definition. Lewis' audience knew what he meant.

His mastery of popular communication partly caused E. L. Allen to accuse him of playing to the gallery. Allen writes: " It is difficult to believe that his arguments would ever win those whom we are most concerned to win, men and women of serious thought and a strong sense of responsibility who seek guidance both for their own lives and for that of society, but who are dissatisfied with traditional presentations of Christianity." [108] Allen has a rather selective audience. This raises again in acute form the question: To whom shall we make apology? The answer for many is "the intellectual elite." And much of classical apologetics is directed to them. Hence, to the intellectual aristocrat, it is the eighth deadly sin to "play to the gallery" and ignore those "whom we are most concerned to win." W. Norman Pittenger accused Lewis of ignoring subtleties, nuances, and ambiguities, and of using vulgar concepts. In reply, Lewis reiterated that he was writing *ad populam* and not *ad clerum*, which is relevant to his manner as well as his matter. He undertook his apologetic task, he contended, because the evangelists and cultivated clergymen were not then reaching the people. He regarded his task as that of a translator of Christian doctrine into language the people could understand. In regard to vulgarity, Lewis replied, "If it gets across to the unbeliever what the unbeliever desperately needs to know, the vulgarity must be endured." [109] Then Lewis threw to Pittenger and to us all the challenge: "How does he himself do such work? What methods, and with what success, does he employ when he is trying to convert the great mass of storekeepers, lawyers, realtors, morticians, policemen, and artisans who surround him in his own city?

"One thing at least is sure. If the real theologians had tackled this laborious work of translation about a hundred years ago, when they began to lose touch with the people (for whom Christ died), there would have been no place for me." [110]

If apologetic defense is confined only to the beachhead attacked by the Twentieth-Century Division of Intellectuals, the enemy will swarm through the ranks of the unscholarly and win the war. It would be indefensible to contend that Christian apologetics should be directed strictly to the masses, and always on their level. But it is equally indefensible that apologetics should be restricted to the academic community, as though the larger world does not exist. Certainly there is a role for the technical language and concepts of a Tillich who writes specifically for intellectuals. But we must never let intellectual arrogance cause us to ignore the masses who could never understand a Tillich but who have agonizingly real questions about religion. For the common reader, Lewis makes the Christian faith a live option. More proficient theologians could do worse.

IV

THE APOLOGETIC METHOD

IN THE CASE OF C. S. LEWIS, his apologetic method is inseparable from its literary vehicle; the Logos (something said) is intimately bound up with Poiema (something made). That fact alone sets Lewis apart from most apologists who have, from a literary standpoint, nothing distinctive about their writings. Many apologists have started with the same Logos as Lewis; few have encased it in such varied or uniformly excellent Poiemai. His content is orthodox and his arguments old, but his unique use of Poiema in the service of Logos, if not new, is at least unusual and refreshing. And the strength of his apologetic is as much, if not more, in its Poiema as in its Logos.

By strict standards of definition, it might be argued that only a few of Lewis' didactic writings are genuine apologies — namely, *The Problem of Pain, Miracles,* and *Mere Christianity.* Of all his writings, only they in a straightforward, discursive manner deal with specific problems in traditional apologetics. But if we accept a broader view of the nature and purpose of apologetics — the view that apologetics takes place on the frontiers of Christian commitment where it attacks modern idols, affirms the existence of the One God and his revelation of himself and redemption of the world in Jesus Christ, and seeks a common ground in reason and experience for leading non-Christians into Christian belief — then we cannot restrict apologetics to academic statements, discursive argument, or logical and scientific systems. J. V. Langmead Casserley surely is correct in arguing that different causes and forms of unbelief require different approaches, and that apologetics might range from simple statements of the Christian rationale to seizing the initiative and attacking specific contemporary forms of unbelief.[1]

From this viewpoint, whatever shakes man's faith in his modern gods, whatever disturbs his sense of security in a closed universe, whatever awakens his longing for ultimate values and God, whatever presents a credible statement of the Christian faith and makes it a live option, whatever pushes man to the razor's edge of spiritual decision — that is a legitimate and useful weapon in the arsenal of apologetics. And if one accepts that broad view of the nature and purpose of apologetics, then virtually everything Lewis has written — his didactic writings, his satires, his space trilogy, his children's stories, his essays and sermons, his devotional writings, and even his scholarly writings — has apologetic value. Christian presuppositions underlie his scholarly writings, and in the midst of any subject it is not unusual for The Evangelist to pop out with a subtle statement of faith and a gentle nudge of the unbeliever toward faith.

We propose, therefore, in our appraisal of his apologetic method (1) to study his use of different literary forms or genres, and (2) to study his forensic techniques and devices. Since our interest is in literary forms and not necessarily in individual books, we shall not make extensive synopses of the books (except where it is illustrative of the literary form) and our selection of books will be illustrative, not exhaustive. Our interest in his literary forms concerns their value and purpose as vehicles of apologetics and not necessarily their value as literature. We shall omit from our study the scholarly works and his poetry only because they have no direct apologetic purpose. We shall try to uncover Lewis' purpose in each form — mythology, children's stories, allegory, satire, fantasy, autobiography, didactic writings, and sermons and essays — and then to estimate its value in breaking through to modern man.

The Literary Forms of Apologetic

Mythologies

Lewis' imaginative writing — alive, inventive, and at times creatively imitative — obviously is swimming against the contemporary literary current. Realism, with its reporting technique and its concentration on the empirical "facts" of everyday life, has dominated modern literature. Both in literary criticism and by writing, Lewis waged unrelenting war on the "bare fact" or "skeleton in the closet" or "slice of life" kind of writing. Lewis contended against the realist: "He is a sham realist. He accuses all myth and fantasy and romance of wishful thinking: the way to silence him is to be more realist than he — to lay our ears closer to the murmur of life as it actually flows through us at every moment and to discover there all that quivering and wonder and (in a sense) infinity which the literature that he calls realistic omits. For the story which gives us the experience most like the experience of living is not necessarily the story whose events are most like those in a biography or a newspaper." [2] Because realism has dominated the recent past, Lewis was forced to write the kind of books he himself wanted to read. And so from his pen flowed a rich variety of myths, allegories, fantasies, and fairy tales.

We have already noted the epistemological importance of myth for Lewis, how it conveys to man reality that cannot be contained in discursive thought. But beyond accepting the value of ancient and modern myths as a way of knowing, Lewis uses the mythical form to convey his own ideas about the world and religion. Myth is encountered at different levels in Lewis — in individual mythical images (like Screwtape, Merlin, Logres, the Grey Town, Cair Paravel, the Utter East), in specific remythologizations of Christian or pagan myths, and in myths encompassing a whole story. Four of Lewis' novels can be classified unquestionably as myths — the space trilogy and *Till We Have Faces*. The children's Narnia books also have a mythological character, but since they are addressed to a different audience, they will be discussed under the heading "Children's Stories."

Lewis intends for his myths, like those of the best mythmakers, to strike roots below the surface of the reader's mind and help him to break out of his normal mode of consciousness. The best myth, he writes, "gets under our skin, hits us at a level deeper than our thoughts or even our passions, troubles oldest certainties till all questions are reopened, and in general shocks us more fully awake than we are for most of our lives."[3] Since a great myth may be conveyed by inferior words, Lewis contends that "the value of myth is not a specifically literary value, nor the appreciation of myth a specifically literary experience."[4] One may delight in the myth and deprecate the literary work, or delight in the literary work and miss the myth. From that standpoint, the value of Lewis' myths is bound up not with their literary quality but with their inherent power to convey mythically some aspect of reality. The added pleasure in Lewis' works is their excellence as literature apart from the myth.

Lewis' selection of the space-time novel as a mythical form was prompted by his reading of Olaf Stapledon's *Last and First Men* and an essay in J. B. S. Haldane's *Possible Worlds*, resulting in the desire to replace their immoral outlook with his own Christian point of view. Lewis had already learned from David Lindsay's *Voyage to Arcturus* that the space-time novel is a valuable literary form for raising questions about man's existence. Lewis writes: "No merely physical strangeness or merely spatial distance will realize that idea of otherness which is what we are always trying to grasp in a story about voyaging through space: you must go into another dimension. To construct plausible and moving 'other worlds' you must draw on the only real 'other world' we know, that of the spirit."[5] The space-time novel is ideally suited both for what Lewis wanted to say and what he could best do; it allows free play for his unique literary skills. In the space novels, Lewis is poet, theologian, philosopher, social critic, teacher, and word-weaver.

Lewis' interest in the space novel is not to tell a story that could be told just as well on earth, or to serve as a medium to convey sheer excitement. Rather, through it he enters the spiritual world and probes the outer and other, the inner and deeper, dimensions of human existence. The utility of the space novel is that it gives an extraterrestrial vantage point from which to view the dilemma of man in the universe. Ransom's experience on the planet Perelandra is Lewis' prescription for modern man: " At Ransom's waking something happened to him which perhaps never happens to a man until he is out of his own world: he saw reality, and thought it was a dream." [6] The universe that Lewis portrays is not outer space but " Deep Heaven "; not a vast, cold, barren, lifeless void, but the created realm of God which is populated by beings analogous to man and by superior beings in the hierarchy of nature. It is not hostile or peopled with the monsters of science fiction, but an unfallen realm where creatures live in love and obedience to God.

Lewis' aim in the space novels is to convey to the reader what Ransom experienced in his travels, " the sensation not of following an adventure but of enacting a myth." [7] At times the novels fall below his mythical purpose and lapse into allegory, if we judge by Lewis' own distinction between myth and allegory. " What shows that we are reading myth, not allegory, is that there are no pointers to a specifically theological, or political, or psychological application. A myth points, for each reader, to the realm he lives in most. It is a master key; use it on what door you like." [8] Lewis does occasionally point in the novels. No one could doubt that Ransom is a figure for Christ, the Green Lady a figure for Eve, and the King a figure for Adam. They are like, yet not the same as, their counterparts. But despite occasional allegorical pointers, the total effect of the novels does convey myth to the mythically sensitive reader, myth that offers a glimpse of the reality behind the appearance of nature and man and claims the lasting allegiance of the imagination.

The space novels have an integrated theme, beginning with *Out of the Silent Planet,* followed by *Perelandra* and finally *That Hideous Strength;* yet each teaches its own lesson. The powerful myths roughly parallel " Paradise *Un*lost," the Garden of Eden, and the Tower of Babel. The adventure begins when the hero of the series, a Cambridge philologist named Ransom, is kidnapped and taken to Malacandra (Mars) by Weston and Devine, who symbolize respectively the scientific technocrat and the greedy adventurer. Having previously been to Mars, Weston and Devine mistakenly believe that the inhabitants of Mars require a human sacrifice. Landing on Mars, Ransom escapes and is pursued by Weston and Devine. Upon meeting the three rational species of Mars, Ransom finds them friendly, peaceful, and sinless. Ransom discovers himself in an unfallen world where the nearest verbal equivalent for sin or evil is " bent." Despite their biological and functional differences, the three species — the *hrossa* (the poets), the *pfifltriggi* (the artificers), and the *sorns* (the intellectuals) — live in harmony and love and in obedience to God. No artificial barrier between the natural and supernatural exists; the natural species have intercourse with the *eldila,* who are something like angels, and with the *Oyarsa,* who is something like the archangel of the planet. Ransom learns that his own planet, Thulcandra, is the " silent planet," cut off from the spiritual life of the universe because of its fallen archangel, the Bent Oyarsa. Ransom for the first time informs the Malacandrans of the Incarnation. His space " eye-view " reveals the fallenness of his own world, the perversity of man's desire for celestial colonization, the misery that man creates wherever he spreads his infection of evil. He discovers that the vast distances of space are God's quarantine protection of the universe against the evil of man — an evil symbolized in the selfishness, greed, and ambition of Weston and Devine as they kill and try to intimidate the Malacandrans. The Oyarsa finally, after many illuminating conversations, dispatches the three earthlings back to their silent planet.

Perelandra is the most hauntingly beautiful and theologically important of the trilogy. Ransom, now in periodic communication with the eldila of Deep Heaven, is supernaturally transported to Perelandra (Venus), where he finds an unfallen Paradise complete with an innocent king and queen, the first new life to emerge on any planet since the Incarnation. Weston soon arrives in his spaceship, and through him the devil invades Venus. So begins the story of Temptation in Perelandra. The Green Lady roughly represents Eve, Weston the Serpent, and Ransom the savior of the planet. What follows is the temptation by Weston, the counterattack by Ransom, the reasoning of the Green Lady about whether to disobey God and leave the floating islands and remain overnight on the Fixed Island. After days of reasoning with the Green Lady, a battle to the death ensues between Ransom and Weston (now the Un-man or Evil Incarnate), culminating in the death of Weston, the escape of Ransom from a subterranean cavern, and the crowning of the King and Queen in Lewis' awesome vision of The Great Dance.

But *Perelandra* is more than a retelling of the Temptation. As Ransom realized, "the parallel he had tried to draw between Eden and Perelandra was crude and imperfect." [9] Reality never repeats itself. The Incarnation altered the universe forever, and the Incarnation was an indirect saving of Perelandra through Ransom. As the Voice said, "It is not for nothing that you are named Ransom." [10] Ransom had become an instrument of God in the spiritual warfare of the universe that reaches a climactic battle in *That Hideous Strength*.

That Hideous Strength, "a tall-story about devilry," portrays the danger Lewis warned against in *The Abolition of Man*. The forces of evil working for the dehumanization of man operate behind a scientific-sociological front organization, the National Institute of Coordinated Experiments (N.I.C.E.). The real purpose of the N.I.C.E. is to take control of human destiny, to create "Man Immortal and Man Ubiquitous," to establish "Man on the throne of the universe." But the N.I.C.E., unknown to its members, is actually the instrument of the Bent Oyarsa of Earth and his cohorts as they invade humanity.

The story is a strange mixture of elements. Beginning with humdrum scenes and persons — a small college, an ordinary married couple, Mark and Jane Studdock, the tedium and ambition of everyday life — Lewis introduces a horrifying social-scientific enterprise that would do credit to Orwell or Huxley — the N.I.C.E. which is directed by the decapitated head of a mad scientist, Alcasan. He then filters in a weird combination of mythical, druidical, and supernatural forces to combat the N.I.C.E. and the Bent Oyarsa. Ransom, the connecting link with the previous space novels, is now the Pendragon, the mystical successor to King Arthur and the head of the spiritual forces opposing the N.I.C.E. Within his previous mythical framework, Lewis incorporates four major elements of Arthurian myth — the perpetual battle between Logres and Britain (spiritual versus secular), the reappearance of the Fisher King and Pendragon in Ransom, and the figure of Merlin.[11] The combination of the Arthurian elements with the conflict of extraterrestrial powers conveys the gravity and magnitude of the issue, which is another chapter in the struggle between Logres and Britain. The trilogy ends with the destruction of the N.I.C.E. and the momentary defeat of the earth's dehumanizing forces.

The space novels, in addition to their mythical function, also serve as mouthpieces for Lewis' theological ideas as well as organs for social criticism. Ransom's discussion with the Malacandrans touches on the problem of pain, death, immortality, the nature of sin, free will, providence, and religion. On Perelandra lengthy dialogue occurs about the fall of man, the incarnation, redemption, and the last things. *That Hideous Strength* contains incisive statements on the nature and destiny of man and the unseen dimensions of our universe. At the heart of the trilogy is the sin of pride, the desire of man to usurp the place of God, the ultimate form of which is to dominate the universe and live forever. His unmistakable conclusion is that God will destroy our modern Tower as surely as he did the Tower of Babel. We will pull down Deep Heaven on our heads.

If it be objected that these are interesting tales but hardly believable and certainly not apologetics, let Lewis reply with his reason for telling the tale in fiction: "It was Dr. Ransom who first saw that our only chance was to publish in the form of *fiction* what would certainly not be listened to as fact. He even thought — greatly overrating my literary powers — that this might have the incidental advantage of reaching a wider public, and that, certainly, it would reach a great many people sooner than 'Weston.' To my objection that if accepted as fiction, it would for that very reason be regarded as false, he replied that there would be indications enough in the narrative for the few readers — the very few — who at *present* were prepared to go further into the matter.

"'And they,' he said, 'will easily find out you, or me, and will easily identify Weston. Anyway,' he continued, 'what we need for the moment is not so much a body of belief as a body of people familiarized with certain ideas. If we could even effect in one per cent of our readers a change-over from the conception of Space to the conception of Heaven, we should have made a beginning.'" [12]

Till We Have Faces, which Lewis regarded as his best book, is a retelling of the classic Cupid and Psyche myth — of Psyche's being tempted to look on the face of Cupid and, consequently, being cursed to wander the earth — with certain significant alterations. Because of its symmetry and complexity, the novel defies brief summarization. Although not explicitly Christian, it is thoroughly religious and through potent symbolism raises questions about man and his relation to the Transcendent. As Lewis retells the myth, it is "the straight tale of barbarism, the mind of an ugly woman, dark idolatry and pale enlightenment at war with each other and with vision, and the havoc which a vocation, or even a faith, works on human life." [13]

Orual, the ugly sister, becomes the focal point of Lewis' myth, the picture of self-deception. Lewis' alteration of the classic myth makes Orual mask her jealousy of Psyche as love and her vision of Cupid's palace as appearance, which modifies the whole character of the tale. Because Orual wore the mask of self-deceit, she could not meet the gods, speak to them, or hear them. Hence, the question of the novel: "How can they meet us face to face till we have faces?"[14]

Lewis fills the novel with contrasting themes — barbarism and enlightenment, beauty and ugliness, appearance and reality, barrenness and fertility, love and hate. Here we encounter the shallowness of rationalism, the curse of selfish love, the necessity of vicarious sacrifice, the mystery of the divine, the necessity of repentance, the "water-spouts of truth from the very depth of truth." *Till We Have Faces* is intellectually powerful and demanding. Lacking the enchantment, beauty, satire, and scientification of the space trilogy, it will be read only by intellectuals. And even they will not digest it at the first reading. For those who succeed in catching the myth, it will raise momentous issues.

Several limitations to the use of myths for apologetics must be faced. As Lewis himself admits, we live in an age dominated by realism, an age barren of the qualities found both in childhood and in the infancy of the race — "that tireless curiosity, that intensity of imagination, that facility of suspending disbelief, that unspoiled appetite, that readiness to wonder, to pity, and to admire."[15] There is a current disparagement of the romantic, the idyllic, the fantastic. But childhood indicates that love of the romantic is a normal and perennial human taste, that it exists where it has not been atrophied by fashion. There are adults who are attracted to imaginative writings. Hopefully, literary fashions will change; when they do, the romantic may again be widely valued.

But another limitation will continue to exist for mythical writing. Myth depends upon the apprehending individual; "the same story may be a myth to one man and not to another."[16]

For that reason we can never be sure what happens when a man reads a book: it may be an exciting yarn to one and convey a myth or something like to a myth to another. Lewis sets down one important qualification for myth: "I have met literary people who had no taste for myth, but I have never met an unliterary person who had it." [17]

So, by his own standards, there would be a great group of the unliterary who would find his space novels merely fantastic, who might enjoy them for their excitement, but who would miss the mythic overtones and never enter into the author's mind or have their deepest questions reopened. The author would have to be more direct, precise, and obvious. And in *Till We Have Faces* they would find only barbarism, blood, and pagan religion — a rather silly tale they would not bother to finish. Yet others will discover stirrings within the depths of their beings that are impossible to put into words. Each to his own taste!

Children's Stories

The scene is a new world at the moment of creation. As a great lion prances around singing a song, the stars and sun appear, and grass and flowers and trees grow up. As the song grows wilder, the grassy land begins bubbling like water in a pot, pouring out humps of earth that turn into different animals. Pairs are selected from among the dumb animals, and in a wild voice the lion cries out: " Narnia, Narnia, Narnia, awake. Love. Think. Speak. Be walking trees. Be talking beasts. Be divine waters." [18] And the pairs of animals begin to talk and the trees begin to walk.

But what is this? A fairy tale? An allegory? A myth? Those animals and trees! Did they begin to talk and to walk, or was it only barkings, growlings, and snarlings, and only the wind in the trees? And that lion! Did he speak, or was it only a roar? Is he a lion, or is he perhaps more than a lion? Not everyone would agree. Digory, Susan, and the Cabby saw the whole miracle of language and locomotion. But wicked Uncle Andrew, by volitional choice, only heard a lion's roar and the noisy din of bloodthirsty beasts. About the Narnia stories as well as the scene of Narnia's creation, "what you see and hear depends a good deal on where you are standing: it also depends on what sort of person you are." [19]

Where one stands determines greatly what he finds in the Narnia books. They may be read as merely exciting fairy tales for children. Or they may be seen as superbly crafted masks for high and noble ideals and for Christian values and theology. Measured by Lewis' own hedonistic standard for literature, the Narnia books delight and give pleasure to anyone who is in the least susceptible to the fairy tale. But the Christian's delight is in more than the books as things in themselves. Although as a general principle, Lewis argued that literature should not be valued for what it says or for the truth it contains about life, we cannot be that aesthetically intent and ideologically unconcerned about these books. However, it is true that they stand at a high level as literature apart from their value as covert statements of the Christian faith.

How good the Narnia books are as literature must be left to the judgment of the children who read them and to the specialists in children's literature. The "experts" rate them highly. Roger Lancelyn Green, an authority in children's literature, ranks Lewis among the half dozen best children's authors of the twentieth century.[20] Charles A. Brady calls the seven Narnia chronicles "the greatest addition to the imperishable deposit of children's literature since the Jungle Books." [21] *The Last Battle* received the Carnegie Medal for the best children's book of 1956. The high level of sales of the books indicates a number of readers among the more literary of children.

The chronological sequence, although not the order of publication, begins with *The Magician's Nephew*, followed by *The Lion, the Witch and the Wardrobe; The Horse and His Boy; Prince Caspian; The Voyage of the Dawn Treader; The Silver Chair;* and *The Last Battle.* The Narnia books, like the space trilogy, take the reader out of this world, and partly for the same reason — that looking back he may see things in his own world he would otherwise never have seen. But here, instead of being propelled into space, the reader is carried into another dimension. Narnia is not another planet in space, but another dimension in the universe. No time correlation exists between Earth and Narnia; a year on Earth might be decades of Narnian time. Passage between the two world dimensions occurs by different devices: magic rings, a magic wardrobe, a picture of a ship, a hole in a schoolyard wall, a railway platform. The chronicles encompass the whole life-span of Narnia but involve only two generations of Earth children — Digory, Polly, Peter, Edmund, Lucy, Susan, Eustace, and Jill — who in different episodes become kings and queens in Narnia and are, on occasion, called back to Narnia, usually when Narnia is troubled.

The stories involve a series of adventures, beginning with the creation of Narnia by Aslan the Lion, the entrance of evil, and the establishment of a London cabby and his wife as the first king and queen. Later, when Narnia is overrun by a host of evil creatures, Aslan offers himself as a substitute for the captive Edmund and is killed on a Stone Table by the White Witch. Aslan resurrects from death, destroys the White Witch and her followers, and crowns Peter, Edmund, Lucy, and Susan as kings and queens. In another episode the children are called to the aid of Prince Caspian, the heir to the throne of Narnia, and help him defeat his uncle, King Miraz, who had usurped the throne. Four children join an exciting adventure on the "Dawn Treader" which, with Prince Caspian, is sailing to the unknown eastern seas and Aslan's own country. *The Silver Chair* creates a horrifying picture of the captivating power of evil in the story of Prince Rilian's imprisonment deep inside the earth under the spell of a wicked witch. The final book tells the end of Narnia, the judgment on evil, and the resurrection and final bliss of Aslan's followers.

The books are delightful as literary creations. There are strange and enchanting countries — Calormen, Archenland, the Island of Darkness, the Island of Death, Telmar, the Giant

City, Underland. There are the dashing and courageous Narnian kings — Caspian, Rilian, and Tirian. There is a large array of vividly depicted creatures — Mr. Tumnus the Faun, Trumpkin the Dwarf, Jadis the White Witch, Reepicheep the valiant Mouse, Puddleglum the Marsh-wiggle, Strawberry the Cab Horse, the Monopods, Shift the Ape, Puzzle the Donkey, Jewel the Unicorn. Lewis draws upon a wealth of mythological and fairy-tale creatures and elements — fauns, satyrs, centaurs, dwarfs, giants, talking beasts, walking trees, gods and goddesses of the woods and rivers. Into his Narnian creation, Lewis pours the characteristics of the real universe — awe and wonder, the aliveness of nature, the intercourse between species, the sanctity of life, the mystery of existence; the magical, divine, ecstatic, terrifying reality in which we live.

Here one encounters the noble values of life and civilization — heroism, truth, beauty, justice, honor, duty, courtesy, self-sacrifice, pleasure, happiness. The reader also, to the objection of sentimental critics, meets violence, bloodshed, suffering, pain, cruelty, and death — facts no less real in the world as we know it. From the Christian perspective, the chronicles cover a wide range of ideas from creation to consummation, including the miracle of creation, the fact of evil, sin, the nature of salvation, incarnation, redemptive death as substitution, and the last things (including an apocalyptic vision of the collapse of the created order). And so the perceptive reader discovers beneath the myth a panorama of the values and terrors of life and a wealth of Christian symbolism. But above all there is Aslan the Lion — the Creator, Redeemer, Consummator. Aslan is no sentimental creation. He is not a tame lion. Although he plays with the children or allows them on occasion to ride him or bury their faces in his mane, he does not allow them to be familiar with him. He is a commanding figure who with little emotion can say, "I have swallowed up girls and boys, women and men, kings and emperors, cities and realms." [22] Aslan is a commanding presence in Narnia — and obviously more than a lion.

THE APOLOGETIC METHOD 155

But from the standpoint of apologetics, the nagging question arises: Do children really get all that out of the stories? And the answer is: Probably not! But that is part of the genius of the stories. Their many ramifications do not limit their reading to childhood. The Narnia books are an important addition not only to the library of children's literature, but also to the rare realm of Christian myth and symbolism. They can be profitably read by adults and will be reread by children after they become adults. It is difficult to know exactly what young readers get from the books. Roger L. Green believes that "naturally an ordinary child's criticism or appreciation turns on the actual adventure, and it is not possible to discover the effect of the underlying allegory or moral inherent in all the stories." [23] If the child finds here only the thrill of adventure, does that fact disqualify the books as apologetic works? Charles A. Brady finds an apologetic value even then: "The child will not respond to these values at once, though they will awaken in his memory when the time comes for full realization. He will respond immediately, however, to the narrative sweep; to the evocation of the heroic mood; to the constant eliciting of the numinous. Very possibly this latter service is the most startling one Lewis renders to contemporary childhood. . . . He touches the nerve of religious awe on almost every page. He evangelizes through the imagination." [24]

If the imagination has been sparked and the nerve of religious awe touched, the child will later come back. In fact, the consequent unfolding of the truth of the stories in the adult years was in Lewis' mind. Adult enjoyment was a criterion Lewis established for good children's books. "No book is really worth reading at the age of ten," he contended, "which is not equally (and often far more) worth reading at the age of fifty — except, of course, books of information." [25] Then why bother to write children's books? Lewis replies, "Because a children's story is the best art-form for something you have to say." [26] Certain ideas go best into that form.

Modern Child is child of Modern Man. And the reason of

Modern Man is corrupted; he is out of touch with the true nature of reality. So Lewis paves one of his roads to the Celestial City with the asphalt of numinous imagination. Thus all the mythological elements — the giants and dwarfs, the talking beasts and walking trees, the White Witch and the great Lion — create an atmosphere and evoke an imaginative response that is impossible with discursive reasoning or didactic writing. They create awe and bewilderment, where one sees, yet does not quite see, some aspect of reality. The fairy tale can help to set before the imagination something that baffles the intellect. And then, having returned from fairyland to the blinding glare of our own world, perhaps — just perhaps — one will see more clearly the deeper dimensions of life.

That, at least, was Lewis' intention. That is the theme and purpose of Narnia. Through a kindling of the imagination, Lewis aspired to bring his readers to God. At the close of *The Voyage of the Dawn Treader,* Lucy pleads with Aslan to allow Edmund and herself to return to Narnia.

" ' Dearest,' said Aslan very gently, ' you and your brother will never come back to Narnia.'

" ' Oh, Aslan! ' said Edmund and Lucy both together in despairing voices.

" ' You are too old, children,' said Aslan, ' and you must begin to come close to your own world now.'

" ' It isn't Narnia, you know,' sobbed Lucy. ' Its *you*. We shan't meet *you* there. And how can we live, never meeting you? '

" ' But you shall meet me, dear one,' said Aslan.

" ' Are — are you there too, Sir? ' said Edmund.

" ' I am,' said Aslan, ' But there I have another name. You must learn to know me by that name. This was the very reason why you were brought to Narnia, that by knowing me here for a little, you may know me better there.' " [27]

Allegory

Allegory, as we have seen, belongs to man in general, for " it is of the very nature of thought and language to represent what is immaterial in picturable terms." [28] Allegory, in that sense, is not to be arbitrarily used as "a better or worse way of telling a story." [29] It serves, rather, a specific purpose. The allegorical method was forced into existence in the latter days of paganism when man's gaze was turned inward. As a literary form, it has been developed in order to paint the inward world and supply the subjective element in literature. It is the way of personification, the creation of *visibilia* to express immaterial facts, emotions, and passions. In contrast to the author of symbolism and mythology, the author of allegory knows exactly what he is talking about, and the allegory is a personification or picture-pointer to some invisible reality. Lewis contends that Dante was right in using allegory as "a piece of technique, a weapon in the armoury of [rhetoric]." [30] From the apologetic standpoint, a skillful allegory can say what might otherwise require a full-scale philosophy of religion. It is not accidental that John Bunyan's *The Pilgrim's Progress* and Dante's *Divine Comedy* have remained perennially powerful statements of religious faith.

Allegorical elements enter into many of Lewis' writings, including at times the space novels, the children's stories, and the satires. His most obviously full length allegory is *The Pilgrim's Regress: An Allegorical Apology for Christianity, Reason, and Romanticism*. First published in 1933 and later revised in 1943, *The Pilgrim's Regress* is unmistakably patterned after Bunyan's *The Pilgrim's Progress*. Building on the base of his own experience, Lewis generalizes about man's spiritual pilgrimage through the world situation of the 1920's and 1930's. Set within the framework of a dream journey, it tells the story of John, a boy in Puritania, who is awakened to sweet desire or the longing for joy by the sight of a distant island and the sound of sweet music. Enchanted, John leaves Puritania in pursuit of the object of his longing. Along the journey he embraces many false objects and confronts many false claims that leave his desire unsatisfied — sex, the abandonment of moral legalism, magic and occultism, science, psychology, various artistic movements, different schools of philosophy, worldly wisdom, human virtue, and much else. Lewis creates some compelling allegorical personifications, among them the Brown Girls, Media Halfways, Mr. Enlightenment, Reason, Sigismund Enlightenment, Mr. Mammon, Master Parrot, Mr. Sensible, Mr. Humanist, and Mr. Wisdom. After numerous side excursions off the main road to the North and the South, John is faced with the inescapable choice of abandoning himself to Mother Kirk. Barred from retreat by Reason, John is taken across the Peccatum Adae Canyon by Mother Kirk who requires him to abandon all efforts at self-preservation and plunge naked into an underground stream. Emerging from the stream as Christians, John and Vertue are given a guide to lead them back to Puritania. For the first time they see the world as it actually is. Every vista is different because they now see their old attractions through Christian eyes.

As literature, *The Pilgrim's Regress* is not among Lewis' best books. In his 1943 Preface to a revised edition, he faulted himself on two counts: his " needless obscurity, and an uncharitable temper." [31] In the 1943 edition he tried to clear up the obscurity by supplying a key to the allegories in a running headline through the book. When, by his own standard, allegory should clearly point, it is a serious defect when a key must be supplied for the allegories. But while many of his allegorical images are indeed obscure, others are incisively drawn.

Despite its defects, the book's importance is not to be disregarded. Much of Lewis' wisdom is there — sharp, biting, satirical — but without the later wit and charm that is characteristic of Lewis. It is one of Lewis' best books for a penetrating critique of various modern movements and thought. With rapier strokes he lays bare the major weaknesses of science, rationalism, humanism, Freudianism, aestheticism, subromanticism, and many others. It should be read for those insights if for no other reason. The truth of the book becomes more profound after the second or third reading. But here, above all, Lewis exposes the reader most clearly to what he means by *Sehnsucht*, the goad of longing that leads man to God, a longing which Lewis believes is within every man. He intends by taking the reader along the footsteps of John to help him see that his frantic grasping of movements, forces, ideas, and biological drives is only a way of avoiding the abandonment of self that is so essential to finding the true object of man's desire — God.

Satire

The Screwtape Letters, Lewis' most famous book, has become a literary classic. Its initial sales were prodigious and are still brisk twenty-odd years later. Leonard Bacon in 1943 called it "the most exciting piece of Christian apologetics that has turned up in a long time . . . a spectacular and satisfactory nova in the bleak sky of satire." [82] The infernal correspondence is a series of letters from Screwtape, an administrative assistant in hell, to his nephew, Wormwood, an inexperienced young tempter on earth, giving him advice on how to undermine the faith of a young man to whom he has been assigned. The shocking and unexpected strategem of looking at everything from the viewpoint of hell results in the book's complete "moral inversion — the blacks all white and the whites all black — and the humour which comes of speaking through a totally humourless *personna*." [83]

Here we again encounter a characteristic apologetic device of Lewis' — the use of a literary medium to help the reader transcend himself and look back in at himself, the world, and God from a different perspective. But here the device is different from the use of space in the space trilogy, or the use of dimension in the children's books, or the use of personification in the allegories; here one gets to look at himself and the world from "below," through the devil's eyes. It is enlightening to stand with the Father Below and trace the spiritual progress of Wormwood's patient from his conversion and joining the church, through the temptations and ups and downs of his spiritual life, until his death in an air raid and his slipping from Wormwood's grasp into the arms of God. And it is startling to see that what from our human point of view is *simpliciter* an innocent or intrinsically good may, with a slight demonic twist, become from the point of view of hell a force working for our damnation.

The technique of inversion allows Lewis freedom to satirize and condemn anything he wants by the simple expedient of having Screwtape praise it; or he may advocate a certain value or practice or belief by having Screwtape condemn it. And the correspondence covers a wide gamut of life and behavior. To accomplish his purpose, Lewis probes the human psyche and levels devastating blasts at certain aspects of contemporary society.

Even his construction of hell is an ingenius satire on the corporate connivings and individual competitions of the Managerial Age. His symbol for hell " is something like the bureaucracy of a police state or the offices of a thoroughly nasty business concern." [34] Lewis' hell has all levels of executives and workers, and it comes complete with a Tempter's Training College, an Intelligence Department, and a House of Correction for incompetent tempters. He pictures a diabolical society held together by fear and greed — fear of punishment in deeper houses of correction within hell, and the greed to dominate and even to devour one's fellows. But the utter self-interest that is hell is concealed by a surface film of suave manners and official respect.

Lewis happened to believe in devils, a fact that has little to do with the purpose of the book. The devils and machinery of hell should not divert the reader from the main concern — the devilment and temptation in the individual heart. Whether they are viewed as concrete realities or as personifications of abstractions is irrelevant, for Lewis' purpose is " not to speculate about diabolical life but to throw light from a new angle on the life of men." [35]

The value of Screwtape as an apologetic work is not in any argument for the existence of devils but in its uncomfortable, disturbing, yet humorous laying bare of an inescapable element of man's existential situation. When one has finished reading the infernal correspondence, he has not heard a reasoned argument for the existence of the devil or the demonic, nor any philosophic or theological statements about the origin or the role of evil or the demonic in the scheme of things. In fact, unless one becomes sidetracked, it is not the devil but himself he has seen. For the apt reader there is no problem of literalism, demythologizing, or remythologizing. Upon finishing the book, the sensitive man, as well as having the funny bone tickled and the conscience pricked, will think: Call it what you may — Tempter or Temptation — here is an undeniable element of human existence, one mysterious aspect of reality itself; I have been on the receiving end of the devious machinations of evil. And then, whatever their ultimate source, all of life's spiritual distractions and perversions — the misuse of reason, the metallic clamor of urban society, the interruption by hunger of serious thought, the deathly grip of habit, the danger of inverting virtues, the tensions of the home, the difficulty of prayer, the stranglehold of anxiety and fear, the perversion of pleasures and sex, the undulations of the spiritual life, the suffocating conformity of society, the destructive effect of ambition, the watered-down religion of the modern church — all these take on new dimensions and are seen as a part of numerous devilish devices that keep one from facing the ultimate question of human existence — the relationship of man to God.

The value of this type of satire does not depend on whether the reader agrees with the satirist at every point, for example, on the dress of women or the attitude toward war. The value comes from the total effect mediated from the book. Satire cannot reach every man. Satire uses humor and, as Lewis says, "humor involves a sense of proportion and a power of seeing yourself from the outside." [86] It requires a willingness to look at oneself, to laugh at oneself, to learn about oneself. That possibility is not open to the devil. Lewis' hell is a place of seriousness, gravity, self-importance, resentment, and concern for one's own dignity. The devil could never laugh at himself and "cannot endure to be mocked." Presumably, there are people so dominated by the demonic spirit that they have lost the capacity for self-transcendence and a laugh at their own expense. But judging from the success of the diabolical letters, here is one satire that has "jeered and flouted" the devil and produced as much repentance as resentment.

Fantasy

The literary genre of *The Great Divorce* is difficult to classify. Within the overall fantasy, it is sermon, symbolism, satire, philosophy, theology — now one and then the other. Again Lewis uses his method of giving the reader an extraterrestrial vantage point from which to view the human situation. For that purpose he adds to his use of other literary devices — space, dimension, personification, the devil's eyeview — a retrospective look at life, its issues and choices, from purgatory or the point of life's termination. Looking back, one learns that life is an absolutely unavoidable either-or, that it presents innumerable small daily choices that culminate in the choice of heaven or hell. For those who have completed the journey, heaven and hell will appear to be everywhere and earth will not appear a very distinct place. The retrospective look will show that "earth, if chosen instead of Heaven, will turn out to have been, all along, only a region in Hell: and earth, if put second to Heaven, to have been from the beginning a part of Heaven itself." [37]

The Great Divorce is a dream-vision, with Lewis as narrator, of a busload of ghosts traveling from the Grey Town (either hell or purgatory) to the environs of heaven. Gripped in the throes of self-interest, they are so drained of their humanity and their substantial selves that they find the terrain of heaven too solid for their flimsy, phantasmal spirits. The grass hurts their feet and the rain bombards them like rocks. Most of the ghosts from the bus are engaged in conversation with a Solid Person who has been sent by God to lead them into heaven. Provided with the opportunity of remaining permanently in

THE APOLOGETIC METHOD 163

heaven, with the exception of a man captivated by lust, they all refuse to abandon their favorite sin and choose to return to hell. With the help of George Macdonald, whom he encounters in the dream, Lewis analyzes the sins, excuses, and root causes of the sins. In the course of their conversations, Macdonald philosophizes on different subjects — the nature of heaven and hell, time and eternity, freedom and predestination, the inevitability of choice.

The humor of Screwtape is absent here; it is deadly serious business, and even the satire carries an aura of gravity. Lewis relentlessly analyzes the psychology of self-will in its manifold disguises and starkly pictures the eternal issues that hang upon individual temporal choices. Here we meet the decent man who rejects companionship with a murderer; an apostate clergyman who holds "honest opinions fearlessly followed"; a cynical ghost; a woman wearing her feelings on her shoulder; a flirtatious female; an artist preoccupied with "art for art's sake"; a wife ambitious for her husband's advancement; a possessive mother; a man dominated by lust; a tragedian intent on making his wife miserable. As surely as he does with Orual in *Till We Have Faces*, Lewis penetrates beneath the masks of his characters to show that self-will and self-love have many faces but only one destination. Beneath the surface sins and excuses of all the characters lies the real problem — self. Their real choice is the old one of God or Mammon, God or self. And beneath their superficial excuses, each is really saying, "Better to reign in Hell than serve in Heaven." [38]

Nowhere else does Lewis underline more forcefully that man is made for more than earth, and that all who miss the joy of heaven do so by their own choice. He shows clearly that heaven and hell are eternally divorced, and that there can be no heaven with even a little hell in it. And heaven and hell depend on the individual choice of self-will or God's will. Toward the end of the dream, Lewis asks Macdonald whether the choices of the ghosts to stay in heaven and abandon their sin or to return to hell were "only the mimicry of choices that had really been made long ago." And Macdonald replies, " Or might ye not as well say, anticipations of a choice to be made at the end of all things? But ye'd do better to say neither. Do not ask of a vision in a dream more than a vision in a dream can give." [39] Through this particular dream, thoughtful readers will learn something about themselves, something about life, and something about eternity. Just as Lewis, before he awakens from his dream, has a moment of terror in which he thinks the judgment has caught him unprepared, so the reader should lay down the book with the haunting question of the possibility that " this night your soul shall be required of you."

Didactic Writings

Since our intention is to analyze and appraise the literary forms Lewis uses, and not every book he has written, three of his books will be selected as illustrative of his method in his didactic writings. The selection of *The Case for Christianity, The Problem of Pain,* and *Miracles* necessarily omits important books like *Christian Behaviour* and *Beyond Personality,* the other two books contained in *Mere Christianity.* It also does not treat books like *Letters to Malcolm, The Four Loves,* and *Reflections on the Psalms* which, although important for the background and range of his thought, are not so explicitly apologetic works. The study of his didactic writings must necessarily be somewhat different from the study of his other literary forms. The Lewis trademark in the didactic writings, apart from his well-known literary characteristics, consists in the way he approaches his subject and how he develops his arguments. Again, our purpose here is not to present a thorough synopsis of the books. We are interested in what he says primarily in pointing out the zigs and zags in his dialectical movement. But a careful examination of their inner development and line of reasoning requires a more extensive treatment of their contents.

The Case for Christianity. The best example of Lewis' " popular " apologetic style is *Mere Christianity*, the composite edition of his B.B.C. radio talks of which *The Case for Christianity* makes up the first two books. In these talks he had the mass British audience in mind, and his language is simple, chatty, and colloquial, enough so that R. C. Churchill charges that " a passage from ' Christian Behaviour ' is exactly similar to the talks given at the end of Children's Hour Prayers; and the vast majority of Mr. Lewis's radio addresses are on the same deliberate childish level." [40] Perhaps the " childish level " has something to do with *Mere Christianity* still being on the paperback " best seller " list.

In *The Case for Chistianity*, as well as in *The Problem of Pain* and in *Miracles,* Lewis reasons before he preaches. Lewis' line of reasoning is dictated by his belief that Christianity makes sense and begins to talk only after one has faced the facts of the universe. He uses a modification of the moral argument for God to establish the fact of the moral nature of the universe, the fact of man's consciousness of moral obligation and moral failure, and the fact of a Power behind the Moral Law. With his own peculiar twist, Lewis uses the moral argument to establish not merely a Lawgiver but also man's guilt before the Law. In other words, Christianity begins in dismay at one's moral failure and one's responsibility before the Power behind the Law. That general purpose guides the line of his argument.

Lewis' process of reasoning, up to the presentation of the " case for Christianity," is neat, tidy, and closely argued. He first states the case for Natural Law, then the objections to Natural Law and his refutation of the objections. The reality of Natural Law raises the question of what lies behind the Law, the question of the nature of the universe. He then presents the choice of available answers — those of materialism, religion, and emergent evolution. Having established the necessity for a religious answer, Lewis states the alternatives: pantheism and theism. The crucial test for any religious view is its ability to deal with the problem of evil; here pantheism, atheism, and liberal " Christianity-and-water " alike flounder. Only two defensible options are open on the question of evil —

either dualism or Christianity. Dualism cannot provide an ultimate source for our distinction between good and evil. So the Christian answer alone remains, and man had better hear the claims it makes. Lewis then states the Christian message and appeals for individuals to choose the right side in the moral conflict.

That is the general thrust of his reasoning, but his arguments at specific points are intriguing and disarmingly simple. For example, he begins his argument for Natural Law (which he calls the Law of Human Nature, or the Moral Law, or the Rule of Decent Behavior) with the practical fact of our appeal to a rule of behavior to settle quarrels, and the further fact that we fail to do ourselves what we expect of others and then make excuses for our failures. From this, two points emerge: (1) All people have a sense of oughtness and (2) all people do not behave as they ought. The Law of Nature is known in all cultures, and widely differing moralities share more likenesses than differences.

Lewis states and argues at some length against cogent objections to the fact of Natural Law. To the objection that the Moral Law is herd instinct, he replies that at times man follows the weaker of two conflicting instincts, for example, in choosing the saving of a drowning person instead of self-preservation. To the objection that it is a social convention instilled by education, he indicates that education transmits both social convention and " truth " and argues that Natural Law is truth because its general principles are acknowledged in all cultures. From this it follows that the Law of Human Nature, unlike what may be the case with the laws of physical nature, is prescriptive and not merely descriptive. It is not the facts of how people behave but the law of how they ought to behave. Attempts are made to explain away its prescriptive nature by arguing that the moral judgment of another is based on personal inconvenience (which is unsupported by experience, because bad is frequently not inconvenient and good is inconvenient), or that decent conduct pays the race as a whole (which is arguing in a circle). So Natural Law is a real thing but not a fact in the ordinary sense — an indication that there is more than one kind of reality.

The reality of the Law raises the question of what lies behind the Law, the question of the nature of the universe. Only two broad explanations, a materialist or a religious, exist. Emergent evolution offers a third alternative, but if it identifies the "life force" as Mind, it is religious; if it argues that something other than Mind "strives" or is "purposive," it gives one the emotional comfort of believing in God without any of the cost of religion. Because materialism is limited to empirical observation and description, it cannot supply answers to ultimate questions; ultimate causes are not open to scientific investigation. The Reality that makes facts could not be a fact among facts in the universe, but it does show itself inside individual men as a moral force urging them to do right.

At this stage of the argument Lewis is still far from the Christian or even a theistic God. But he has established the need for a religious view of the Power behind the Law and the universe. Two evidences of God are available: the universe he has made, and the Moral Law he has put within. Lewis reduces the rival conceptions of God to two: pantheism and theism. Pantheism teaches that God is beyond good and evil, and that he animates the universe. Theism teaches that God is good and that he invents and makes the universe. The decisive test for a religious viewpoint is the adequacy of its answer to the problem of evil. Pantheism can only ignore the distinction between good and bad. Atheism, if it admits the evil in the world, is too simple because, if there is no God, it cannot explain where we get the idea of just and unjust. Liberal Christianity-and-water is also too simple because, although recognizing the fact, it ignores the seriousness of evil and the Christian judgment on evil.

Only two views, in Lewis' judgment, face the facts. One is dualism, which asserts that there are two independent, opposite powers at war with each other. Lewis thinks that next to

Christianity, dualism is "the manliest and most sensible creed on the market." [41] But to assert, as dualism does, that one of the powers is good and the other bad is to introduce a third standard of judgment which would turn out to be God. Lewis contends that evil is a parasite; it is derivative; it is perverted good. For that reason Christianity has always said that the devil is a fallen angel. Christianity does come close to dualism in declaring that there are two powers at war with each other; but it views it as a civil war, a rebellion by a dark power against God, a dark power who has occupied this world.

The Christian explanation for evil is that God created beings with free will, which alone makes joy, love, and goodness worth having. The evils in our world result from man's abuse of his free will, his wanting to be like God, and his attempt to invent happiness outside of God. God cannot give man happiness apart from himself. Our captivity to evil is the key to history's calamities. Lewis paints a graphic picture of God making a divine invasion into this "enemy-occupied territory" through the conscience, dreams and myths, the election of Israel, and, finally, in the incarnation. Jesus claimed to be God and to forgive sins, a claim that makes him a madman, a demon, or else what he said he was. To call him a good moral teacher is not even an alternative. From this point on, Lewis states the orthodox Christian message about the work of Christ, with special emphasis on his death; the nature of the Christian life; and the way the Christian life is spread through Baptism, belief, and Holy Communion. He concludes that the God who came once in disguise will come again in force, a coming that will be both terrible and beautiful, depending on the individual's decision about Jesus Christ. Since at the coming of Christ in force it will be too late, the time to choose the right side is now.

The Problem of Pain. This is among Lewis' best books. Charles Hartshorne considers it to be "vigorous, acute, and honest; and if I think that here and there it is badly reasoned, I should think the same of many secular discussions of similar topics." [42] The book states with such extraordinary brilliance

THE APOLOGETIC METHOD 169

and clarity the traditional solution to the problem of pain that it is tempting to quote extensively some of its more luminous and trenchant passages. Not the least of the book's merits is its graphic and fresh restatement of some perennial principles on God's omnipotence, goodness, and freedom; on human sin and the Fall; and on the nature of heaven and hell. In *The Problem of Pain*, as in *Miracles*, a particular problem provides a springboard from which Lewis expounds a wide variety of theological ideas.

As usual in his discursive writings, Lewis first erects an overall philosophic and theological framework before dealing with the problem of pain itself. Any solution demands that the question be placed in a proper context. Pain is not so much one of the problems that must be fit into religion; rather, only from the standpoint of religion, and in particular Christianity, is there a " problem " of pain. Only when man is faced with the dual facts of a suffering world and a loving God does pain become a moral problem; otherwise it is merely one of the facts of existence that we stoically accept. For that reason, atheism, if based on the injustice and suffering in the universe, is a bogus argument. If religion is only the product of man, atheism has difficulty explaining how the idea of a good God has been derived from the spectacle of a universe full of pain and misery. In a sense, our very raising of the question itself indicates that religion derives from a source outside nature. Lewis suggests that there are three strands of religion: (1) the numinous, (2) the universal awareness of moral law that is both approved and disobeyed, and (3) the identification of the numinous power with the guardian of morality to which men feel obligation. Christianity adds a fourth strand — the historical event of Christ — which unavoidably raises the problem of reconciling an ultimate and loving purpose with the suffering and evil in the world, of explaining how a good God can make a bad world.

Lewis gives a classic formulation to the problem of pain: " If God were good, He would wish to make His creatures perfectly happy, and if God were almighty He would be able to do what He wished. But the creatures are not happy. Therefore God lacks either goodness, or power, or both." [43] The thesis Lewis develops to answer this dilemma is that within the total drama of creation, the Fall, and redemption — that is, given the character of God, the nature of creation, the freedom and sin of man, and the ultimate redemptive purpose of God — pain may be a net and complex good working toward what is ideally best for man. The acceptance of such a difficult thesis requires that we define certain equivocal terms about God, that we understand the intended and the actual state of creation, and that we perceive the nature and consequences of sin and evil.

Lewis begins by showing that " good " and " almighty " and " happy " are equivocal terms. In regard to omnipotence, the self-contradictory is absolutely impossible even for God. In creating the world, God accepted certain limitations on his absolute omnipotence: the limitations of a relatively independent and inexorable nature, of fixed laws of cause and effect, of a social field in which individuals meet, and of the freedom of the individual will. To exclude the possibility of suffering in a world of free wills and independent nature is to exclude life itself. Similarly, divine goodness and human happiness must be envisaged as being different from what we might normally imagine. The only happiness God can give is the happiness he originally intended, the happiness that results from man's living in submission and obedience to God himself. Unfortunately, man does not know what happiness he should choose. So God's goodness requires that he labor to remove the rebellious stains within our character and help us find our place in the scheme of things. Therefore, love may cause pain to its object, not happiness, if the object needs alteration to be fully lovable or happy.

And man as we know him needs alteration. The solution to the problem of pain can ignore the present state of man no more than it can ignore the nature of divine omnipotence and goodness. Christianity takes it for granted that men are bad, as a result both of the Fall and of individual choice. The Fall had biological as well as social effects, so that man lost control over his organs and was besieged by disease, senility, and death. The point " is simply that man, as a species, spoiled himself, and that good, to us in our present state, must therefore mean primarily remedial or corrective good." [44]

Now directly approaching the problem of pain, Lewis suggests that perhaps four fifths of human suffering results from human wickedness itself. To propose that good now is primarily remedial or corrective good, Lewis admits, is an incomplete answer. But there one must start, for proper goodness and happiness come from the creature surrendering itself to its Creator. As rebels who must lay down our arms, we experience grievous pain in the very act of surrendering our self-will. And yet, paradoxically, the act of self-mortification, which is itself a pain, is made easier by the presence of pain in its context in three ways: (1) Since most humans will not begin to surrender themselves as long as things are going well for them, pain provides the bad man with the opportunity for amendment. (2) Pain shatters the illusion of self-sufficiency, the illusion that what we have, without God, is enough. (3) Pain also helps man toward perfect self-surrender, which must be done purely for God's sake and contrary to our desires. Lewis goes on to make a number of other interesting suggestions about the meaning and purpose of suffering.

The pain experienced by creatures with free wills is two-edged; it may embitter or enrich, depending on the recipients. It can lead either to rebellion or to self-surrender. The inevitable working out of that choice is either heaven or hell. God is so full of mercy that his Son dies that men might be redeemed, but his redemptive purpose will be defeated by those who refuse to be redeemed. Only in accepting the possibility of defeat can God respect the freedom he has willed for men. Hell is God abandoning men to their own desire for freedom. But for those who choose God and self-denial, the sufferings of this present world are counterbalanced by the joys of heaven.

And so, the best that Lewis claims to do is to make credible the doctrine of being made perfect through suffering; he cannot make it palatable. He does not provide a complete answer to the problem of evil, but he does show how God can make complex good out of simple evil, how accepted suffering and repented sin can lead the rebellious soul to his Father and home. As in most of his apologetic books, his overriding accomplishment in this "theological" discussion is to underline starkly to Everyman the imperative necessity of choosing God.

Miracles. Critical reaction to this book has ranged from commendation to calling it "one of the worst books ever written on this subject." Oddly enough, much harsh criticism springs from the refusal of exacting critics to exercise their judgments within the limits Lewis set for himself in the book. The title of the book, *Miracles: A Preliminary Study,* qualifies his purpose. The book is a philosophical inquiry into the possibility of miracles, and as such is only a preliminary to empirical or historical inquiry or to providing a definitive solution to every problem related to miracles. His concern with individual Biblical miracles is not to establish their historicity but to exhibit their innate fitness within God's total purpose. Since he is speaking to the common reader, his definition of miracle is intentionally popular and crude and lacks theological precision. To forget these self-imposed limitations is to subject him to unfair criticism.

Lewis' purpose requires that he establish two facts: the existence of a Power beyond the natural order, and the possibility of that Power breaking into the natural order. The course of his argument is very simple, although he takes numerous side excursions along the way. The first section of the book is devoted to an attack on naturalism. For simplification, Lewis reduces all philosophical and theological metaphysical views into two broad divisions: naturalism and supernaturalism. The naturalist believes that nothing exists outside of nature, that nature is the "whole show" or "everything," a vast interlocking system that goes on of its own accord and has no cause but itself. The supernaturalist believes that someone or something exists outside of nature. Using the rational and moral arguments for the existence of God, Lewis demonstrates why naturalism fails: it cannot explain either reason or Moral Law. Rational thought and valid moral judgments cannot be the products of nonmoral, nonrational nature; they require God as an Ultimate Cause.

Both reason and morality point to the existence of God, but this says nothing about what kind of God he is or how he is related to the world. Naturalists could believe in a certain kind of God. Actually, there are three choices about the relation of God to the world. Either nature produces God, or God and nature are completely independent, or God produces nature. After showing why pantheism and dualism fail to explain the facts of mind and morality and the relation of God and the world, Lewis contends that only theism can provide an adequate view of a God who creates nature and upon whom nature is dependent.

Given that relationship between God and nature, Lewis demonstrates that neither the character of nature, in its dependent role, nor the character of God excludes the possibility of miracle. In regard to nature, he argues that no current view of natural law excludes the possibility of miracles. The popular view that physical laws are necessary truths, which initially seems so formidable, in fact demands that if the supernatural is operating, miracles should occur. In defining miracles as " an interference with Nature by supernatural power," [45] Lewis does not mean that miracle breaks the laws of nature. " The divine art of miracle is not an art of suspending the pattern to which events conform but of feeding new events into that pattern." [46] Once the new event enters nature, it is assimilated into the natural process and obeys all of nature's laws. But miracle is not interlocked backward with nature. It is an event that nature in and of itself could not produce; its cause is God.

The other objection to miracle, that God's character prohibits his invading nature, cuts at the heart of Christianity, which is precisely the story of a Great Miracle. At this juncture in the argument, Lewis devotes a long chapter to the problems that naturalism raises for the frankly supernatural Christian faith with its primitive world view and its anthropomorphic conception of God. In discussing the nature of metaphorical language and the importance of personal images, Lewis uses a distinction between thought, imagination, and speech to separate the core from what is inessential in the faith. But unlike the demythologizers, he contends that it is the core which is miraculous and that "the accounts of the 'miracles' in first-century Palestine are either lies, or legends, or history." [47] Again, he is speaking about miracles in general and not about any miracle in particular, which is a historical question.

Since Christianity is the story of a Great Miracle, our only problem is to establish the propriety of, and a standard of probability for, miracles. Assuming that God controls the universe, Lewis argues that there is a higher harmony and uniformity of nature than we have discovered. The apparent interruption of the orderly course of nature by a miracle may be a vital part of the total movement when measured by the rules beyond the rules. Indeed, miracles may be the very chapters on which the story of the universe turns.

Admitting that miracles happen very rarely and that most accounts are probably false, Lewis contends that a criterion of intrinsic probability becomes necessary by which to judge any particular miracle. The criterion Lewis selects is also the main criterion for our belief in the uniformity of nature — "our innate sense of the fitness of things." He suggests that the fitness and credibility of all miracles depend upon their relation to the Grand Miracle, the incarnation of Christ who unites God and nature. From the perspective of the incarnation, he then discusses the New Testament miracles as miracles of the old creation and miracles of the new creation. "I contend," he writes, "that in all these miracles alike the incarnate God does suddenly and locally something that God has done or will do in general. Each miracle writes for us in small letters something that God has already written, or will write, in letters almost too large to be noticed, across the whole canvas of Nature. They focus at a particular point either God's actual, or His future, operations on the universe. When they reproduce operations we have already seen on the large scale they are miracles of the Old Creation: when they focus those which are still to come they are miracles of the New. . . . Their authenticity is attested by the *style*." [48]

Miracles does have its defects. (1) There is a structural defect in that, despite the simplicity of the general argument, the reader is not always sure where he is in the course of the argument. (2) When adverse criticism repeatedly occurs at points where Lewis has explicitly qualified his intentions, it leads to the suspicion that his qualifications are not clear enough. (3) There is a feeling that beyond demonstrating the "fitness" of particular miracles, he is at the same time tacitly admitting their historicity — which has led to his condemnation for ignoring Biblical criticism. (4) The charge of quasi-deism, although unjustified, results from isolated extravagant statements, which are not immediately qualified, about God breaking into nature from "outside." Yet he is clear that God is also present within the created order. (5) A more serious objection from a scholarly standpoint is that his popular definition of miracle, though admittedly helping him deal with the common reader's questions, does not sufficiently cover the realm of Biblical miracles. Besides the "new events" being fed into the natural process, often a natural event, a propitious occasion, and a sensitive interpreter combine to create a miracle.

The book is at its best in specific points of the discussion and in the overall case it makes for the supernatural and the possibility of miracles. Within its stated limitations it sets forth a credible case. Its major defect is in the blurred signposts along the discursive path.

Sermons and Essays

In addition to writing novels and theological works, Lewis was an essayist and a preacher. He frequently contributed to journals and lectured to special interest groups, and on occasion he preached. Some of his essays and sermons have been collected and published in *Transposition and Other Essays, The World's Last Night and Other Essays,* and *They Asked for a Paper.* Many other essays can be read only in the journals where they first appeared. His essays are incomparable. Always provocative, they are masterful examples of breadth of scholarship, elegance of phrase, and urbanity of temperament. They are perceptive in thought and inimitable in style — a tangy mixture of intellect, imagination, and humor in which epigrams flow freely from his pen and metaphor after metaphor is flung at the reader with effortless ease. As a critic suggested, to examine the arguments in his essays is like watching a master chess player who makes a seemingly trivial and unimportant move that turns out later to have been a stroke of genius. Some of the essays reveal how thin is the dividing line between literary criticism and theology. Christian theology hovers like a cloud over even the essays that are primarily concerned with literary criticism, and periodically it irrupts like a flash of lightning.

Many of the essays deal in one way or another with the relevance of the Christian faith and values in the twentieth century. Some of the essays in *They Asked for a Paper* offer incisive critiques of the contemporary world. Lewis' inaugural lecture at Cambridge, "*De Descriptione Temporum,*" is his most ambitious attempt to place contemporary civilization in a proper historical perspective. "Lilies That Fester" portrays the putrifying effect of culture and the threat it makes to Christianity when it becomes an end in itself. "The Inner Ring" exposes one of the deepest motivating factors and corrupting influences of society and one of the major problems for Christian apologetics. "Psychoanalysis and Literary Criticism," especially in its epistemological reflections, is as valuable for the theologian as for the literary critic. The problem posed for Christian vocation in a world of calculated mediocrity that no longer produces good products is confronted in "Good Work and Good

Works," contained in *The World's Last Night.* "Screwtape Proposes a Toast," also in *The World's Last Night,* is a potpourri of social, political, educational, cultural, psychological, and religious criticism of the twentieth century.

Other of his essays are notable for their Christian content and the questions with which they grapple. The nature of theology, of imagination, of world models of thought, and the validation of the Christian faith are discussed in " Is Theology Poetry? " in *They Asked for a Paper.* Several essays in *The World's Last Night* confront problems spotlighted by our modern situation. " The Efficacy of Prayer " faces the difficulties involved in believing in the causal efficacy of prayer. An essay delivered to the Oxford Socratic Club, " On Obstinacy in Belief," takes a new look at the relation between faith and knowledge. " Religion and Rocketry " suggests tentative answers to some sticky questions raised for the Christian faith by the space age and our interplanetary exploration. " The World's Last Night " presents a statement of Christian eschatology that challenges our modern evolutionary historical presuppositions, cuts through Biblical symbolism to the bare minimum of " truth," and on that basis summons modern man to spiritual decision.

Lewis' sermons, preached usually in university churches, have a higher intellectual content than the Broadcast Talks. *Transposition and Other Essays* contains the limited number of his sermons available in published form. Several of these are also included in the other two books of collected essays. Each deals with an important subject and attempts to translate difficult and abstract theological concepts into meaningful and understandable language and application. But they are not " popular " preaching. Horton Davies thinks that writing and broadcasting are happier mediums for Lewis than is preaching. " In them Lewis is a chained falcon," says Davies, " however high he may occasionally soar." [49] Nevertheless, even if they have a defect as " popular " preaching, the published sermons will remain important as oracles for several fundamental ideas.

"Learning in War-Time" deals with the everyday life of the Christian, with the necessity of serving God by doing the ordinary things of life in a Christian spirit despite crises and the distraction of world events and anxieties. Lewis' most thorough treatment of the nature of the church as the body of Christ, of its organic character as opposed to collectivism or individualism, is in "Membership." The suggestion has already been made that "Transposition" represents one of Lewis' greatest contributions to theological thinking. The most eloquent and moving of all Lewis' sermons is "The Weight of Glory," a memorable statement of the nature of man's immortal longing and what his goal entails. Three of these sermons — "Membership," "Transposition," and "The Weight of Glory" — are of lasting importance, particularly if taken at the level of apologetics instead of preaching. Yet, however taken, they illustrate Lewis' use of still another literary form in the defense and proclamation of the Christian faith.

Autobiography

Spiritual autobiography has traditionally been a powerful apologetic instrument. When discursive reasoning or fertilizing the imagination or preaching fails, here is always another "rabbit in the hat." "Let me tell you what happened to me —" was an apologetic device of the apostles, an auspicious instance being Paul's defense before the Jewish mob in Jerusalem (Acts, ch. 22). The apostles proclaimed a historic fact, but they also disclosed a personal encounter with that Fact. The same recounting of personal spiritual experience has produced such monumental works as Augustine's *Confessions,* John Bunyan's *Grace Abounding to the Chief of Sinners,* John Henry Newman's *Apologia pro vita sua,* or Albert Schweitzer's *Out of My Life and Thought.*

Lewis' spiritual autobiography, *Surprised by Joy,* covers his life up to the time of his conversion. It spotlights his central experience of *Sehnsucht* and deftly traces the twin paths of his pilgrimage — the dialectic of reason and the dialectic of imagination — as they converge in the Incarnate God Jesus Christ. Lewis' literary skill allows the reader to live through Lewis' own spiritual experience and, hopefully, to find himself at certain junctures along the journey. Here Lewis discusses the reasons for his attachments to certain movements and philosophies. And here he does not systematically argue against them; he simply explains why he personally found them inadequate. Nor does he attempt to demonstrate or argue for the validity of his religious experience; he merely describes it — articulately, dispassionately, but earnestly. One cannot rationally " prove " the fact of *Sehnsucht* in human experience, that heaven is our true home and God the Object of our longing, or that the Object, the Key to the mystery of life, can be found while riding in a car on the way to a zoo. But the believer who finds any rapport with Lewis' experience may find himself believing in a testimony what he would refuse to believe in a treatise. Just as the best advertisement for a soap product is the next-door neighbor who has used it and not necessarily a television commercial giving all the reasons for its superiority, so the most persuasive argument for the Christian faith may not be in a book of discursive reasoning but in the life of one who has tried the Christian prescription and found that it cured his disease, his sickness unto death. *Surprised by Joy* is a masterful example of evangelization through autobiography, and a fitting capstone to his literary defense of the Christian faith.

Devices and Techniques of Debate

A difficult, practical problem for the average Christian is how to engage the non-Christian in discussion and lead him to the Christian faith. Whether confronting a skeptic, a hostile antagonist, or a seeker, Christians often feel inadequate and ill-prepared. Many average Christians, both in pulpit and in pew, can profitably appropriate from Lewis some simple methods and techniques to use in defending their faith. Having examined his apologetic purpose in various literary forms, we will now turn the spotlight on his prominent devices and techniques of debate, without special reference to types of literature, in order to gain a composite picture of his apologetic method. The actual apologetic confrontation involves essentially three elements: the attack on non-Christian viewpoints, the defense of the Christian rationale, and the attempt to transform intellectual acceptance of the Christian faith into personal commitment to the living God.

The Attack

Perhaps the most critical aspect of the apologetic confrontation is that of attacking and demolishing the arguments of the opposition. Because of its importance, Lewis' facility in attacking the opponent's arguments will be examined in more detail than his method of defense and presentation of the Christian faith (which have already been examined more thoroughly). The apologist must initially break down the defenses of his opponent either by refuting his arguments, shaking the foundations of his thought, raising doubts about its validity, or exposing its inadequacy. Lewis throws a variety of weapons at his opponent — ranging from tossing not strictly logical bombs to engaging in close combat within the arena of logic.

Not Strictly Logical. Substantial criticism of Lewis has resulted from his skillful use of nonlogical means to attack his opponent's arguments or ideas — ranging from satire through sarcasm, caricature, dyslogistic personification, and on to outright evasion of the issue. He was not infrequently accused of lacking charity, or of giving in to the temptation to bang those stupid unbelievers over the head, or of a lack of sympathy and compassion for his opponents, or of smug self-righteousness about his own viewpoint. Part of that tendency must be seen in the light of his deliberate forensic effort to puncture the balloon of non-Christian pomposity and deflate the superiority complex of contemporary naturalism. " Anything is fair in love and war." And Lewis was at war against the forces of unbelief.

The master of satire always runs certain risks. He may make his point by humor, ridicule, and exaggeration, and yet offend his opponent. Not everyone is responsive to satire simply because it demands a capacity for objectivity. Some people get from satire a laugh at their own expense; others only bristle. Lewis is at his best when using meticulously controlled satire that lets us see the foibles and follies of humanity — in the individual, in society, and in the church. Mark Studdock, a glob of sycophantic putty, satirizes mass conformity. Belbury's manufacturing of the news slashes newspapers, as Experimental School does modern education. Modern scholarship is the target of the Historical Point of View, noncritical thinking of the Spirit of the Age, and liberal Christianity of Christianity-and-water.

On occasion Lewis is bluntly sarcastic. With a few strokes of the pen, he can cut deeply whatever he dislikes — from public life to theological views. He warns that ordinary people go among naturalistic liberal clergymen as sheep among wolves. He can slap at J. A. T. Robinson by saying that God's immanence must be emphasized among deists, then caustically adding, " — or perhaps in Woolwich, if the laity there really think God is to be sought in the sky." [50] Sarcastic venom drips when Mr. Enlightenment explains scientific induction to John: "to use popular language, if you make the same guess often enough it ceases to be a guess and becomes a Scientific Fact." [51]

Just as comedy may run from rib ticklers to slapstick, Lewis at times expands his satire to the point of caricature — which can be both an advantage and a handicap. Latent tendencies and hidden flaws within a person or a movement are easily seen in caricature. Weston, for example, is a disturbing caricature of the technocratic scientist; Devine, of the greedy, speculative adventurer; the N.I.C.E., of the dangers of our budding scientific-governmental bureaucratic combine. And they are gross distortions, but through them Lewis would hope that the caricatured could see the flaws and irregularities of their own profiles and take remedial action. Satirical caricature can backfire. Lewis has been accused of unfairly stating an opponent's position so that the views he presents of naturalism, or the historical quests, and other opposition viewpoints are not close enough to be photographs; they are strictly caricatures. He is setting up straw men to serve as his whipping boys. In rebuttal to that accusation, it may be argued that Lewis does indeed occasionally oversimplify, but he never intentionally distorts the essence of an opponent's view. He implements in writing what we have learned from the impressionists in painting: that the most accurate picture of a given subject is not necessarily a photograph.

Personification is another of Lewis' prominent characteristics. The personifications are so vividly drawn that no reader can forget them. In them the psychologist in Lewis is busily at work. Some of the personifications are explicitly allegorical, including the whole cast of unforgettable characters in *The Pilgrim's Regress* — characters like Sigismund Enlightment, Mr. Humanist, Mr. Wisdom, Mr. Mammon, and Master Parrot. Many memorable characters in Lewis' writings are little more than personifications of attitudes that nevertheless can be given appellations — Mrs. Self-Concern, the Tragedian, the Ambitious Wife, the lecherous Lizard of Sensuality, the Flirtatious Female, Mr. Cynic, and many others. The inner psychological and moral world is opened up by the personifications. Often Lewis will turn a mild word into a dyslogistic tool that preconditions the reader before he has read the argument by the simple device of capitalization. One has a mind-set against the Innovator, the Conditioner, the Style-Monger, or the Materialist Magician before ever discovering what he believes. The personification itself, the impression connoted by the appellation, is as integral a part of his argument as his logic.

The not strictly logical devices already mentioned, if kept under tight reign, can justifiably be used by an apologist. But on rare occasions Lewis resorts to a forensic " gimmick " that does him no credit and detracts from his usual carefully reasoned work: he evades a question while giving the appearance of answering it. He covers up a sickly argument with a flowery phrase. The best-known example of evasion is his treatment of atheism in *Mere Christianity*. It is so clever and succinctly stated that the spice conceals the poor meat. He begins by contending that atheism cannot explain how we got our idea of just and unjust without an ultimate standard of justice, which is God. But then he unobtrusively shifts from talking about justice to talking about meaning. And he concludes: " Consequently atheism turns out to be too simple. If the universe has no meaning, we should never have found out that it has no meaning: just as, if there were no light in the universe and therefore no creatures with eyes, we should never know it was dark. *Dark* would be without meaning." [52] " *Touché*," says the admirer. " Bosh," says the logician. There is no logical parallel in this way between injustice and nonmeaning. Further, to require the same degree of evidence for nonmeaning as for the assertion that the universe has no discernible meaning is nothing more than word juggling. Here is a subtle, carefully disguised but age-old evasion of the laws of rationality — a variation of the *argumentum ad ignorantiam*. What he is really saying is: " The universe has meaning because you cannot prove it has no meaning; it would be impossible to prove it has no meaning unless a standard of meaning existed by which to measure nonmeaning. The standard of meaning makes nonmeaning impossible." And that, as Lewis must have known, is logically utter nonsense.

Nonlogical Factors in Unbelief. There is an interesting paradox in Lewis' approach to logic. Because of his intense commitment to the use of reason, he deplored the use of the *argumentum ad hominem* in debate, feeling that it is fatal to rational discussion; and yet he uses it surprisingly often in his own writings. The *argumentum ad hominem* generally directs the attack toward the speaker rather than toward what is said, so that its simplest form would say, " This statement is false because you are a certain kind of person or because you are captive to something else." Lewis uses variations of the *ad hominem* to reveal the illogical factors — psychological, emotional, social, intellectual, environmental, even diabolical —

which lie behind many non-Christian viewpoints. The redeeming factor is that Lewis uses it not to evade rationality but to make rational discussion possible, not to discredit the opponent's argument but to clear the air for a rational examination of the opponent's arguments. As a logical fallacy, the *argumentum ad hominem* evades the laws of rationality; as a tool of Lewis, it helps discover the laws of rationality and force the opponent to reason.

"Bulverism" is the name Lewis gives the form of the *ad hominem* that he rejects — the substitution of psychological explanation for logic. Lewis regards his imaginary inventor of Bulverism, Ezekiel Bulver, as one of the makers of the twentieth century. Bulverism, of course, is a parody of the Freudian method of substituting psychoanalysis of the opponent for refutation of the opponent's arguments, the method of explaining all ideas as the expressions of psychological needs. Bulverism assumes without discussion that the opponent is wrong, then busily explains how he became so silly. Thus capitalism, communism, Christianity, and all other outlooks can be dismissed because they are assumed to express some psychological, social, or economic need of their adherents. "Until Bulverism is crushed," Lewis contends, "reason can play no effective part in human affairs." [53]

Despite his rejection of the validity of the method, Lewis uses it on the Freudians themselves by showing that there are equally good psychological reasons for the atheist's disbelief in God or the moral relativist's rejection of an absolute Moral Law. Because there is fear-fulfillment as well as wish-fulfillment, there are four possibilities in the religious predicament. "A man may be a Christian because he wants Christianity to be true. He may be an atheist because he wants atheism to be true. He may be an atheist because he wants Christianity to be true. He may be a Christian because he wants atheism to be true. Surely these possibilities cancel one another out?" [54] Bulverism is a truly democratic process. It works both ways. So while deploring its epistemological validity, Lewis finds it of utilitarian value in establishing a *détente* with the Freudian so that psychological scarecrows are not used by either side.

An aversion to Bulverism does not prevent Lewis from at times attacking the inner and outer nonlogical causes of unbelief with the intention of forcing the reader to ask whether his views have a reasonable basis. One way is to illuminate how many attitudes and ideas have a psychological and not a rational basis. Jane Studdock's hesitancy about religion is linked to her fierce psychological need for independence. " Don't commit yourself to anything," she tells herself. " You've got your own life to live." [55] Much of Mark Studdock's thought had been adopted in order to please his teachers or to ingratiate himself with his colleagues. Why? Mark " liked to be liked." The apostate clergyman in *The Great Divorce* just started saying the kinds of things that won applause. Emotional trough periods sporadically can compel even Christians toward unbelief. In numerous places Lewis illustrates the deep psychological and emotional aversion to the ideas of a transcendent God, an absolute Moral Law, a creaturely status before the Creator, and an inescapable either-or in life. So Christian liberals " want the gilt-edged security of a religion so contrived that no possible fact could ever refute it." [56] Emergent evolution seeks the emotional comfort of religion without any of the cost. And the pantheist does not have to worry about the Transcendental Interferer.

Another inner cause of unbelief is the perversion of man's reason. Ratiocination can become an end in itself. " For me there is no such thing as a final answer," says the apostate clergyman who delights in arguing for the sake of arguing. " The free wind of inquiry must *always* continue to blow through the mind, must it not? . . . To travel hopefully is better than to arrive. . . . There is something stifling about the idea of finality." [57] There in graphic terms is Lewis' picture of a congenital preference for the hunt but an aversion to the kill. And congenital preferences are obviously not rational.

As repeatedly observed, Lewis regards contemporary man as so shaped and controlled by forces outside himself that he is in danger of being reduced to a cipher. The individual's ideas and actions are largely determined by the inner rings, the Culture Monger's Central Bureau, the democratic process, society at large, and various political, economic, educational, and social institutions. The Spirit of the Age and the Climate of Opinion tend to homogenize the masses and to curtail independence of thought or the free play of reason. By his assault on the Climate of Opinion, Lewis waves a series of red flags, hoping to shock the reader into a rational reexamination of his thinking to see whether it is based on reason or absorbed osmotically from the contemporary atmosphere.

Lewis' metaphysical outlook — his very real belief in the warring of spiritual forces in the universe — gives him another almost devious instrument with which to stimulate the reader to a reexamination of his outlook. Might there be, he leaves us asking, not only inner and outer but also supernatural causes of unbelief? Audaciously, he asserts that our modern skepticism about the devil's existence is one of the devil's chief accomplishments. Assuming that temptation is real, Lewis pictures Screwtape encouraging certain fallacious viewpoints — materialism, the abandonment of careful logic, emergent evolution, undue faith in science, or the Historical Point of View. The diabolical advice is given, obviously, with tongue in cheek. But it might shake a person's confidence in his own rationality to think he possibly may have been beguiled by the Tempter.

The real purpose in Lewis' attacking the nonlogical factors in and behind his opponent's ideas has nothing to do with logic. He merely tries to force the opponent to a self-examination, to ask whether he is being rational or whether he has become the hapless victim of his own emotions, of his psychological or intellectual needs, or of the pressure of society and the Spirit of the Age. He is clearing the air of cobwebs in preparation for rational engagement. Then he confronts his opponent with philosophical and historical arguments — which alone can determine the truth or falsity of religious or non-religious claims.

The Apologist and His Opponent. Lewis confronts his opponent's arguments in a variety of ways, with the particular approach being governed by the credibility of the argument and by what is required for refutation. Being committed to the use of reason, he usually attempts to state an opposition viewpoint as fairly and clearly as possible. Then, as a general rule, he grants as much truth as possible to the opponent's argument; but in making concessions, he cautions about the possibility of conceding too much. To acknowledge a core of truth in certain theories or ideas is not the same as granting all the details or implications of the opponent's view. In our overeagerness to allow the enemy any advantage he can fairly claim, "we are liable to overshoot the mark and treat him too kindly." [58] It is possible to eliminate what is integral to the Christian faith.

Lewis sometimes latches on to the opponent's arguments and uses them to his own advantage or turns them against the opponent. With devastating effect, he employs the Freudian wish-fulfillment theory against Freudianism itself. When naturalism asserts that the Biblical cosmology is mythological, Lewis adopts the same line of reasoning to expose the vast myth at the heart of the contemporary scientific cosmology and to establish that any world model, religious or scientific, primitive or modern, must necessarily be mythological in character.

Disdainful, blunt rejection sometimes replaces his more kindly treatment of an opponent's argument, particularly when it is based on historical ignorance. In dialogue with someone who has his historical facts wrong, Lewis may suggest, "Let us not talk nonsense." In the same vein, he may dismiss an erroneous statement of ancient beliefs and ideas by charging, "That is a lie." Or in *The Pilgrim's Regress* he indicates that provincialism produces some fallacious views. "That is always the way with stay-at homes," says the hermit History. "If they like something in their own village they take it for a thing universal and eternal, though perhaps it was never heard of five miles away." [59] All of Lewis' approaches to his opponent's arguments move the discussion inexorably into the arena of logic.

The Arena of Logic. The first rule of logical debate is to attack the strong point of the enemy. " Every good general, every good chess-player," Lewis writes about God's redemptive use of death, " takes what is precisely the strong point of his opponent's plan and makes it the pivot of his own plan." [60] That observation governs Lewis' logical assault on the manifold citadels of unbelief. Whether dealing with Freudianism, materialism, atheism, dualism, or whatever, he does not waste time with sniping action or raiding remote outposts; he assaults the enemy command post. Deliberately refraining from an extensive assessment of all the minute pros and cons and implications of a non-Christian viewpoint, he usually isolates and attacks its main argument. If General Headquarters can be defeated, he reasons, the privates in the field will wither from a lack of coordination.

This stratagem is vividly illustrated in Lewis' exposure of the fatal self-contradiction at the very heart of naturalism. The naturalistic evolutionary myth depends upon inference from observed facts, and inference depends upon reason. But the naturalist asks us to believe that reason is the unforeseen and unintended by-product of the aimless process of mindless matter. Lewis' approach to non-Christian viewpoints is wrapped up in his comment on this contradiction. " After that," he says, " it is hardly worth noticing minor difficulties. Yet these are many and serious." [61] A similar battle plan unfolds in his confrontation of emotive ethics, logical positivism, atheism, and many other views.

Often Lewis will lay bare his opponent's presuppositions, especially when the opponent begs the question and merely assumes what he sets out to prove. Numerous examples of his deft skill in handling question-begging arguments have been noted, among them Hume's assumption of the uniformity of nature, emergent evolution's secret belief in progress, empiricism's exclusive empirical criterion for truth, or Biblical criticism's belief in the impossibility of prediction. A particularly striking illustration is his observation that two mutually contradictory astronomical speculations about life in the universe have been used as arguments against God. In an earlier day when it was thought that the universe was hostile to life beyond earth, our solitariness was supposed to show the absurdity of believing in God. Now that Fred Hoyle and others contend that the universe is well stocked with inhabitable planets, our lack of uniqueness is supposed to show the same thing equally well. Plainly, one cannot have it both ways. The astronomical argument against God is a remarkable example of utilizing a scientific theory to buttress a religious outlook, of concluding exactly what has been previously decided. The truth is that either astronomical argument has already presupposed that God does not exist so that either theory can be used as evidence.

Another of Lewis' lethal weapons of destruction is what might be called " apologetics by translation," which is done in one of two ways: either by translating a poetic-philosophic statement into cold, hard prose, or by dramatizing the logical outcome of a viewpoint being advocated. By the " translation " Lewis implies, " Here is what is said, but here is what it means." Or, " Here is what is said, but here is where it leads." It is interesting to compare Lewis' translation of highly symbolic language into plain prose with the logical positivist's method of translating into " equivalent sentences " for the purpose of increasing our understanding of sentences.

The best example of translation into cold, hard prose is in a lengthy conversation between Weston and Oyarsa in *Out of the Silent Planet*. The imaginative, fuddled, pseudophilosophic language of Weston is incomprehensible to Oyarsa, so Ransom translates his speech into understandable terms. A brief exerpt will serve our purpose. In explaining to the archangel of Malacandra why earthlings have the right to colonize his planet and even kill its inhabitants, Weston orates:

" ' Our right to supersede you is the right of the higher over the lower. . . . '

"'Life is greater than any system of morality; her claims are absolute. It is not by tribal taboos and copy-book maxims that she has pursued her relentless march from the amoeba to man and from man to civilization.'

"'He says,' began Ransom, 'that living creatures are stronger than the question whether an act is bent or good — no that cannot be right — he says it is better to be alive and bent than to be dead — no — he says, he says — I cannot say what he says, Oyarsa, in your language. But he goes on to say that the only good thing is that there should be very many creatures alive.'" [62]

A major purpose of *That Hideous Strength* is to provide Lewis a medium to portray the hideous implications of certain glibly advocated academic theories, to dramatize where they lead. Frost and Wither and the N.I.C.E. are the eye-openers for the brilliant, young, armchair sociologist Mark Studdock. As Frost attempts to force Mark to achieve complete objectivity and to understand that all motives are "merely animal, subjective epiphenomena," Mark discovers the logical outcome of his own shallow materialism. "The knowledge that his own assumptions led to Frost's position combined with what he saw in Frost's face and what he had experienced in this very cell, affected a complete conversion. *All the philosophers and evangelists in the world might not have done the job so neatly.*" (Italics mine.) [63] At the end of the book Mark recalls that every single doctrine practiced at Belbury had been advocated in earlier pre-N.I.C.E. days by some lecturer at Bracton College. "Oh, of course," writes Lewis, "they never thought any one would *act* on their theories! No one was more astonished than they when what they'd been talking of for years suddenly took on reality. But it was their own child coming back to them." [64]

Another favorite device of Lewis is to spotlight the inability of non-Christian views to answer some obvious questions about life. All materialist systems break down at the problem of knowledge, shackled by an inability to explain the ultimate source of reason or of moral law. All nontranscendental systems fail at the point of morality: they speak in terms of "oughtness" although they have eliminated all transcendental grounds for "oughtness." Idealistic systems provide noble aims, but not the capability for noble living. "Idealism can be talked, and even felt; it cannot be lived." Liberal Christianity ignores and is unable to explain the rough, hard facts of life — the facts of evil, sin, and death. On and on Lewis goes, pointing up the inadequacies and unsolvable difficulties in all non-Christian systems. He believes that any adequate view of the reality in which we live must reasonably illuminate all aspects of that reality.

And so Lewis always aims at engaging his opponent in combat inside the arena of logic. His working hypothesis is that if reason is rigorously applied to his opponent's arguments, the opponent will be forced to look at the case for theism, and, finally, to hear the claims of the Christian faith. So, on the attack, Lewis exerts every effort to break down his opponent's defenses, to reveal his hidden presuppositions, to expose the fuzziness of his thinking, to illuminate possible nonlogical causes of his belief, to dramatize the logical implications of his viewpoint, and to underscore his inability to provide a comprehensive answer to the dilemma of human existence. Then once the opponent finds himself empty-handed and defenseless, he must hear Lewis' case for theism.

The Defense

A question that is difficult to resolve is whether Lewis' architectural and building ability is as efficient as the wrecking machine he employs. Sydney J. Harris writes: "Like so many of his opposite numbers in the Enemy Camp (Shaw, for instance), Lewis is at his best doing mass-demolition work. He can skilfully expose the intellectual fuzziness of his opponents, but the majority of his own constructions seem painfully contrived. Like most fine polemicists, he has a negative capability which is not matched by any originality of conception." [65] The judgment of whether his constructions are contrived depends largely on the mind of the person doing the judging. If one is receptive to natural theology and to the authority of the Scripture and church tradition, then Lewis' constructions, far from being contrived, are highly credible. A lot depends on what kind of spectacles one looks through. A Watusi beauty queen would not, presumably, cause too many hearts to flutter among the pygmies. The two tools he uses in making the case for Christianity are reason and imagination.

The Use of Reason. "I am a rationalist," Lewis said. Successive rungs on his rational ladder to God were, first, the existence of God, then the necessity for theism, and, finally, the superior claims of the Christian faith. Traditional arguments for the existence of God were credible to Lewis. The rational and moral arguments in particular are pegs on which he hangs the theistic position. Recurring repeatedly in his writings, they form the backbone of *The Case for Christianity, The Problem of Pain,* and *Miracles.* The arguments have already been examined in the study of his didactic writings. Lewis states the arguments clearly, simply, and as attractively as they could be stated. Elton Trueblood thinks Lewis has picked up Kant's rather awkward statement of the moral argument and developed it into "a really convincing argument" in *The Case for Christianity.*[66] His presentation of the rational argument, as found in *Miracles,* for example, is difficult to improve upon. Occasionally he slips in the argument from design, for instance, when he argues that the uniformity of nature or the laws of nature require a Legislator to guarantee uniformity.

The value in Lewis' use of the traditional approaches to the existence of God lies in his refinement and originality of presentation and not in any substance of argument. Apart from the freshness of expression, the reasoning has the same virtues and faults inherent within any system of causal reasoning. That these are convincing arguments for many people is attested to by the Roman Catholics and the many Protestants who find them logically persuasive. That they are not logically coercive is attested to by the many who remain unconvinced despite familiarity with the arguments. But for those who are receptive to this kind of thinking, they are exemplary models of the arguments.

Lewis also uses an interesting form of the ontological argument. It differs from the Anselmian original because Lewis centers the argument in man's desiring, not in his intellect. In fact, he said that the dialectic of desire in his own experience, the false roads that he took and the goal he finally reached, forced him "not to propound, but to live through, a sort of ontological proof." [67] Man's consciousness of a desire that no natural happiness can satisfy is an indication that we are made for another world. "Creatures are not born with desires unless satisfaction for those desires exist." [68] Our desire for Paradise is an indication that it exists and that at least some men will enjoy it, just as man's hunger proves that he comes from a race that eats and inhabits a world where eatable substances exist. The ontological argument, along with the other "proofs" for God's existence that Lewis propounds, is most persuasive not to those who are confirmed in unbelief but to the man who believes or is on the verge of belief, to those who are alive and aching with desire. But Lewis uses them initially to establish the existence of God.

Once the existence of God is tentatively established, comparative religion becomes important for determining what kind of God there is. All religions, for Lewis, have grasped something of revelation, but theism alone can stand the scrutiny of reason. When carefully examined, pantheism, dualism, and deism all prove inadequate. Something like theism, at the worst, must be less untrue than any other viewpoint. And once theism is accepted, one cannot ignore examining the claims of the Christian faith. In comparing Christianity to other religions, its similarity to them as well as its distinctiveness from them is important in establishing the validity of the Christian religion. If Christianity is assumed to be true, then the parallels indicate that it is the fulfillment of the hopes and dreams and myths of other religions. There are glimpses, although incomplete, of divine truth in other religions, but the difference between them and Christianity is not between truth and falsity. The great difference is that Christianity claims historical factuality and finality for what in the nature religions is cyclic and confined to the realm of myth and ritual. The incarnation is myth become fact.

The claims of the Christian faith are historical. The truth of Christianity stands or falls with whether or not what the Bible says about Christ really happened. As we have seen, Lewis accepts the essential historical reliability of the New Testament and regards the nonmetaphorical statements as being about events that were empirically verifiable. But Lewis must not be regarded as naïve because of that assumption. He is well aware that historical factuality is not absolutely verifiable, and that it depends upon observers, selection, and interpretation of the facts. Although he contends that whether what Christianity claims really happened is a historical question, he also asserts that we must not deceive ourselves about the degree of verification it can provide. His criterion for the historical probability of the Christian faith is that we demand only the kind and degree of evidence "which you demand for something which, if accepted, illuminates and orders all other phenomena, . . . which at one stroke covers what multitudes of separate theories will hardly cover for us if this is rejected." [69] The final proof of the Christian faith is the comprehensive answer it provides to the heterogeneous questions of life, questions left unresolved by the scientific view alone. " Christian theology can fit in science, art, morality, and the sub-Christian religions. The scientific point of view cannot fit in any of these things, not even science itself. I believe in Christianity as I believe that the Sun has risen not only because I see it but because by it I see everything else." [70]

The Use of Imagination. Lewis' defense of the Christian faith also depends upon the imagination, which he uses in two ways. As a literary instrument, it supplies the verbal symbols and picture language for his writing. As an aspect of man's experience, in the sense of *Sehnsucht,* it provides a point of apologetic contact with the reader. His use of imaginative writings has been examined. But his literary technique, even in his didactic writings where he relies so heavily on reason and logic, also depends for its impact on the myths, allegories, metaphors, analogies, epigrams, and illustrations provided by his imagination. His imagination makes his language and ideas come alive as he creates new metaphors or revivifies old metaphors to help the reader perceive his meaning.

Extensive examples of Lewis' rich supply of verbal symbols and picture language could be given, but they have been sufficiently noted. It is more important here to grasp how he also uses romantic imagination in the sense of *Sehnsucht* as a deliberate approach to his reader. *Sehnsucht*, the longing or desire for the Joy which is God, is found in practically all his books at one place or another. Lewis assumes that the desire for God is smoldering in the breast of every man — as aching, longing, wanting; as joy or, equally, unhappiness or grief; as an indescribable sense of estrangement — and that the desire is often fixed on false objects that leave it unsatisfied. It has much in common with Augustine's insight: " Lord, thou hast made us for thyself, and our souls are restless until they find their rest in thee." Lewis ardently tried to make man aware of his desire, to help him see its false attachments, and to aid him in finding the true Object.

In one of his sermons, " The Weight of Glory," Lewis explicitly admits what he does more subtly in so many places — that he is trying to rip open " the inconsolable secret " in his audience, the secret desire for a transtemporal, transfinite good. After speaking wistfully of " the scent of a flower we have not found, the echo of a tune we have not heard, news from a country we have never yet visited," he writes: " Do you think I am trying to weave a spell? Perhaps I am; but remember your fairy tales. Spells are used for breaking enchantments as well as for inducing them." [71]

Lewis, then, deliberately kindles the fires of the imagination to help his reader discover that he was made for, and in fact longs for, God. He wants his own writings to be one of God's bellows to blow upon the half-dead coals of longing in his readers' breast. And his writings are designed not merely to bring the reader to intellectual awareness of *Sehnsucht* in his own experience but, by the sheer beauty of the writing and the probing of man's secret wants, to create in the reader what Lewis himself first experienced in the glimpse of a flowering currant bush. Nowhere are Lewis' words more touched with ethereal enchantment than when he writes about *Sehnsucht*. Here, deep calls to deep. Out of the primordial origins of the race, out of the history of mankind, out of the secret, inner life of every man, Lewis hears a melody which he sets to the music of literature, and sends wafting across the waves of time the siren's call of eternity. He wants his reader not only to think but to feel: " 'Here at last is the thing I was made for.' We cannot tell each other about it. It is the secret signature of each soul, the incommunicable and unappeasable want, the thing we desired before we met our wives or made our friends or chose our work, and which we shall still desire on our death beds, when the mind no longer knows wife or friend or work. While we are, this is. If we lose this, we lose all." [72]

Lewis speaks to the reason but he touches the soul. And both are important, because man is a thinking-feeling being. But the apologist cannot stop here. When man realizes he was made for more than earth, when he has been rationally brought to see the futility of all non-Christian systems, and when the wholesale creeds have begun to fail him, he is then ready to hear the *Evangelium*, the good news of Jesus Christ.

The Gospel

The modern era differs religiously from the Apostolic Age in that the early Christian preachers could count on a sense of guilt and a consciousness of deserving the divine anger among the people. Thus the Christian message was the *Evangelium*, the good news. All this has changed, so that Christianity now has to preach the diagnosis before it can present the cure. The current overemphasis on kindness to the exclusion of other virtues and the popular effect of psychoanalysis, particularly the theory of inhibitions and repressions, are the two main causes of the absense of a sense of guilt. So a man's vices are excused if "his heart is in the right place." And a sense of shame is regarded as a bad thing — an attitude that breaks down one of the ramparts of the soul.

The knowledge of broken law, Lewis holds, must precede any religious experience. A problem for the apologist who is interested in personal commitment as well as intellectual persuasion is, therefore, how to create a sense of sin in his hearers. Until men feel bad, they lack the first condition for understanding what Christianity is all about. Since preaching against sins like drunkenness and unchastity no longer awakens guilt in many modern unbelievers, Lewis suggests that we must make them aware of having broken the moral law "in quite different directions. We must talk of conceit, spite, jealousy, cowardice, meanness, etc. But I am very far from believing that I have found the solution of this problem." [73]

In actual practice Lewis used a variety of approaches. He repeatedly appealed to the universal awareness of Natural Law to establish the grounds for guilt in man's sense of oughtness and in his sense of not doing what he ought. But in dealing with particular sins, he concentrated most on sins of the spirit. Part of Lewis' genius is his ability to find the spiders of sin lurking in such unlikely places. The psychological vignettes that pervade his writings are often designed to help the reader find the undiscovered sin in his secret closet. He focuses attention on the misuse of virtues or the perversion of love or the thinly disguised vices in our lives. He paints situations and characters that portray subtle sins — self-love, domestic hatred, the "gluttony of delicacy," cowardice, the pride of decency, devilish ambition, and on and on. In so many of his characterizations Lewis tries to cover the gamut of spiritual sins, hoping that somewhere the reader will see himself in the picture. But beyond seeing merely psychological or social defects in himself, the reader must understand that these represent ultimately his sin against God himself. Only when he has some rational acceptance of the Legislator behind the Law can he feel a consciousness of moral guilt in any transcendental way. And only when he feels that he deserves the wrath of God does the Christian faith become credible.

Having preached the diagnosis, Lewis presents the cure. The prescription contains no new medicine nor any new combination of elements. It is an old pill for an old ailment, but it contains everything prescribed in the Scripture and in traditional orthodoxy. Before a person can truly decide, he must hear the true gospel. Part of the rejection of Christianity in the modern era, in Lewis' judgment, has resulted from the caricatures of the faith that have been passed off as the real thing — the infantile pictures of popular religion or liberal Christianity's dilution of the hard and difficult doctrines of the faith. Convinced that there are no oversimple answers to complex spiritual questions, he attempts to communicate the full gospel. What he presents, to be sure, is a *skandalon* to modern man, not in Bultmann's "purer" demythologized sense, but in the sense of being a scandal to the intellect that is conditioned by naturalistic empiricism as well as to the pride of man's spirit. And here it is, Lewis says, the old story of creation, redemption, and consummation; of incarnation, cross, resurrection, and ascension; of faith, hope, and love; of angels and heaven and devils and hell; of the urgency of decision and the eternal finality of temporal choice. Here is the good news, the gift that is absolute demand, the answer to the problems of existence. Accept it and live; reject it and die! There is no third way!

Critics have accused Lewis' presentation of the gospel of being crudely literalistic, uncritical of tradition, unsympathetic to modern thought, and rigidly dogmatic. His commitment to traditional orthodoxy does not mire him, however, in simpleminded naïveté. His presentation of the gospel is something of a paradox. He speaks in an authoritative manner, and yet he honestly admits the doubts and the relative degree of certainty in the Christian faith. Demonstrative certainty would not allow for faith. Faith is to be aware of all the possibilities that God does not exist and yet to reject them. And he admits that there are times when the Christian faith seems highly improbable. But he reminds himself that as an atheist there were times when it seemed highly probable. Lewis contends that one can never be a sound Christian or a sound atheist until he can tell his moods where to get off.

Lewis himself was no stranger to doubt and uncertainty. As he bared his soul in *A Grief Observed*, he revealed how upon the death of his wife his faith collapsed like a house of cards, how the gamble for God becomes serious only when the stakes are high, how the darkest nights of the soul come to the greatest saints. But he shows how out of the logic of personal relations a certainty grows that the Christian faith is the ultimate answer to the human dilemma, and that if it were — inconceivable as it is — not true, then the universe holds nothing else of comparable value. " The Giants and Trolls may win, but we die on the side of Father Odin."

Perhaps Lewis' most poignant and moving dramatization of this is in *The Silver Chair* where the Witch, the Queen of Underland, is attempting to weave her spell over Puddleglum the Marshwiggle, Eustace and Jill, and the Prince, as she says, " Come, all of you. Put away these childish tricks. I have work for you all in the real world. There is no Narnia, no Overworld, no sky, no sun, no Aslan." And Puddleglum replies: " Suppose we *have* only dreamed, or made up, all those things — trees and grass and sun and moon and stars and Aslan himself. Suppose we have. Then all I can say is that, in that case, the made-up things seem a good deal more important than the real ones. Suppose this black pit of a kingdom of yours *is* the only world. Well, it strikes me as a pretty poor one. And that's a funny thing, when you come to think of it. We're just babies making up a game, if you're right. But four babies playing a game can make a play-world which licks your real world hollow. That's why I'm going to stand by the play world. I'm on Aslan's side even if there isn't any Aslan to lead it. I'm going to live as like a Narnian as I can even if there isn't any Narnia." [74] How like another who long ago said, "Lord, to whom shall we go? You have the words of eternal life."

As a preacher of the good news, Lewis does not rest content with confronting the intellect or stirring the imagination or even in presenting the gospel. To know the gospel without knowing God is not enough. So Lewis pushes the reader to the point of spiritual decision. He has an uncanny ability to know what is going on in the mind of his reader at a given moment. He knows that no sale is ever made without a closing, without getting a name on the dotted line. And on occasion he can give an invitation as effectively as any tent evangelist. Life's unavoidable either-or confronts one in almost all of Lewis' writings. Heaven or hell hangs on the decision. Man must daily take into account the inevitable consummation of the universe, a time when it will be too late to choose. "That will not be the time for choosing; it will be the time when we discover which side we really have chosen. Now, today, this moment, is our chance to choose the right side. God is holding back to give us that chance. It will not last forever. We must take it or leave it." [75]

An Evaluation

Only the passing of time can reveal which of Lewis' many literary forms will remain formidable apologetic mediums. As exemplary models of lucidity and logical dialectic, his didactic writings have exalted reason in a reason-disparaging age, made orthodoxy respectable in an increasingly unorthodox age, and have spoken with simple eloquence in an era of theological abstraction. "No Christian living," comments Horton Davies, "is able to bring abstract concepts dancing into life as he has done." [76] As such, the didactic writings have provided strength for many nonintellectual believers and a challenge to decision for many unbelievers. For thousands of Christians he does what he claims as an apologetic purpose: he answers for our uneducated brethren the foibles and errors of the attacks of unbelievers on the Christian faith. The fact that the writings say what many less talented Christians would like to say may yield a clue to their popularity within the church. It may well be that the books allow ordinary Christians the thrill of vicariously participating in Lewis' apologetic triumphs, as well as providing rhetorical weapons to carry into apologetic battle without feeling an overwhelming sense of inferiority in the face of the firepower of the Enemy.

It would be difficult to deny the contention that the impact of didactic writings such as *Mere Christianity*, *The Problem of Pain*, and *Miracles* depends as much on the minds that read them as on the writings themselves. The degree and kind of doubt or unbelief in the reader — whether he is a spiritual seeker, a doubting inquirer, a sophisticated skeptic, whether he is educated or uneducated — determines largely what he finds here. Most conservative Christians find that Lewis states eloquently what they would like to state and gives an " intellectual respectability" to orthodox positions; hence, they find the didactic Lewis logically coercive and literarily scintillating. Most liberal churchmen accuse Lewis of theological "sleight-of-hand" tricks on behalf of an outmoded and irrelevant tradition that gloss over its weaknesses and make the old ideas glimmer and glow with simplicity and attractiveness; hence, they find him dangerous.

It would appear that although the didactic writings are highly appealing to certain types of minds, for the skeptical, critical, questioning seeker they are weakened (despite their obvious value) by the tendencies to oversimplify difficult issues, to cover a weak argument with a felicitous phrase, to evade while giving the appearance of answering an objection, and to contrive an either-or which does not exhaust the genuine logical alternatives. And for anyone who is not receptive to the moral or rational arguments for God, they are hardly persuasive at all. Perhaps for the troubled, questing, intellectual skeptic or churchman there is more appeal in a Bultmann or a Tillich than in the didactic Lewis. One reason for that may be, as Lewis suggests about theological liberals, that they are willing to make more concessions and measure theology by the Spirit of the Age, while Lewis measures the Spirit of the Age by orthodox Christian theology, which to many modern men seems somewhat bigoted, narrow-minded, and intolerant. And Lewis' unwillingness to compromise or "bend an inch" militates against him with some readers. For that reason his didactic writings are devoured by some and rejected by others.

Lewis' imaginative writings, however, have the advantage of being able to avoid some of the pitfalls of his didactic writings. For one thing, they are not hampered by his occasional theological weakness, his ignoring Biblical criticism, or his sometimes too simple approach to difficult problems. In addition, they have the strengths inherent in their varied literary forms and provide a more flexible medium for a sharper criticism of society, a deeper probing of the human psyche, a more imaginative presentation of theology, and an opportunity for wit and humor and numinous imagination. As apologetic instruments, Lewis' imaginative writings — the space trilogy, the Narnia books, Screwtape, *The Pilgrim's Regress*, and *The Great Divorce* — may prove in the long run to be as powerful as, if not more powerful than, his more "orthodox" apologetic writings. The imaginative writings are designed to short-circuit temporarily modern man's inveterate empiricism and force him to discover new channels into the heart of Reality. Lewis provides different imaginative ships — mythology, allegory, satire, fantasy, fairy tale — in which temperamentally different readers may elect to sail through the seas of naturalism to their spiritual New-found-land. Imaginative writing opens exciting possibilities for the apologist.

In the space novels, for example, Lewis intends not to convey a body of knowledge, but to familiarize people with certain ideas, to effect a change in modern thinking from the idea of space to the conception of heaven. At that he does an exceptional job. The space novels allow him to reach a possibly otherwise unreached audience. In a Chicago airport bookstall, a space enthusiast might pick up a copy of *Perelandra* to read some science fiction, and by the time his plane has landed in Los Angeles he has been surreptitiously handed a modern mythologization of Christian theology. In these novels he can read and have questions raised about his "modern outlook" and hear some Christian answers, whereas he might never have entered a church or read *Mere Christianity* or *Miracles* unless he had a prior interest in the Christian faith.

The children's novels also best illustrate the indirect apologetic approach. As we have noted, experts in children's literature insist that the Narnia books are among the finest children's stories of the twentieth century. And in their unique way, they are valuable apologetic forms. Lewis contends that most modern children are barren deserts that need emotional and imaginative watering. The lives of modern children are indeed busy, group involved, and planned by adults, with little opportunity for solitude and privacy. Most of them spend more time with the TV than with books, and their imaginative lives are more familiar with the adventures of Popeye than with traditional fairy tales. They have had nature dissected and its mysteries scientifically explained by professors in classrooms of the air, and they are prematurely conditioned to naturalistic presuppositions in their childhood years. For these modern children, Lewis' novels can serve as a potent introduction to the idea of transcendence, of unseen, nonempirical reality, of the possibilities of life transcending the natural order, of a God who creates, redeems, preserves, and consummates in the form of a Golden Lion in another world. It is difficult to know the mind of a child, but key ideas planted in childhood ought to bear fruit in later life. Who has not been influenced by nursery tales and fairy tales learned in childhood? Who cannot remember the moral of "Snow White and the Seven Dwarfs" or "Alice in Wonderland" and give it deeper significance as an adult? In our metallic, quantitative era, there is value in learning of the sanctity of nature and life and of respect between the species.

But, most of all, we would hope that having encountered Aslan in Narnia, the child would find him by another name in his own world.

If this is getting theology in the back door, it may be one of the best instruments to reach the reading public in a post-Christian era where men do not attend church or have enough interest to read a Bultmann or Tillich or even a didactic Lewis. It just may be that the best hope of reaching many modern unbelievers is not in the obvious knock of the Christian salesman at the front door, but in the subtle, covert knock at the rear. As an apologist, Lewis "plays for keeps." He enters battle with a variety of weapons and attacks from all directions, and if he cannot slay with the spear, there is always the crossbow. Too many of us dare to enter battle with only a knife.

After one has read Lewis, what finally stands out above all else is really not literary style or Christian orthodoxy or matchless scholarship or sparkling wit or dancing imagination. What may be a more powerful apology than any of his books or arguments is the irresistible impression that here, here in this controversial British don, is a man consumed with what the existentialists call *Sorge*, care or concern. But the *Sorge* is not so much for himself as for all men, including the nameless masses who are so defenseless against the forces of unbelief. Here is a man who is utterly convinced of the necessity of choosing for Christ in this vale of decision. Consequently, he could not debate spiritual truth as an academic exercise or spend time splitting theological hairs or worrying about whether the Christian faith can be accommodated to the naturalism of our present era. Of those who do, he asked, "Have we no Other to reckon with?" [77] It might be argued that while he was so skeptical of the present climate of opinion, he accepted on authority the Christian climate of opinion of an earlier era. It might be argued that his ideas are shopworn, or his type of orthodoxy outmoded, or his logic poor, or his understanding of mythology and metaphor too literal, or his attitude to his opponent too harsh and uncharitable, or his arguments superficial, or that his gospel presents an unnecessary *skandalon*. But it cannot be argued that Lewis was unconcerned.

And as Lewis said of Paul, here is something that matters more than writing. Here is a man — generous and sometimes petulant, humble and sometimes proud, perceptively Christian yet not without a hangover of Oxonian upper-middle-class prejudices, logically demanding but at times evasive, a scholar with few close friends, an apostle to humanity, a sinner, a saint — a man who finally lets through " what matters more than ideas — a whole Christian life in operation — better say, Christ Himself operating in a man's life." [78] Perhaps in the case of this fellow Lewis, the atheist turned evangelist and apologist, we learn what really we have known all along — that the best argument ever invented for the truth of the Christian faith is the argument that walks in shoes. Lewis once said that when the idea of Charles Williams and the idea of death met in his own mind, it was the idea of death that had to change. In the same way, when the idea of not-God and the idea of Lewis meet in a sympathetic mind, it is the idea of not-God that must change. Lewis himself is his finest Christian apology.

NOTES

I. The Apologist

1. R. C. Churchill, "Mr. C. S. Lewis as an Evangelist," *The Modern Churchman*, Vol. XXXV (Jan.–March, 1946), p. 336.
2. *Ibid.*, p. 342.
3. Margaret Masterman, "C. S. Lewis: The Author and the Hero," *The Twentieth Century*, Vol. CLVIII (Dec., 1955), p. 543.
4. Clyde S. Kilby, *The Christian World of C. S. Lewis* (Wm. B. Eerdmans Publishing Company, 1964), p. 187.
5. W. Norman Pittenger, "Apologist Versus Apologist," *The Christian Century*, Vol. LXXV (Oct. 1, 1958), pp. 1104–1105.
6. Alistair Cooke, "Mr. Anthony at Oxford," *The New Republic*, Vol. CX (April 24, 1944), p. 579.
7. Tom Driberg, "Lobbies of the Soul," *The New Statesman and Nation*, Vol. XLIX (March 19, 1955), pp. 393–394.
8. Cf. the contrasting views of A. B. Bruce, *Apologetics: Christianity Defensively Stated* (Charles Scribner's Sons, 1904); Alan Richardson, *Christian Apologetics* (Harper & Brothers, 1947); W. Norman Pittenger, *Rethinking the Christian Message* (The Seabury Press, Inc., 1956); and J. V. Langmead Casserley, *Apologetics and Evangelism* (The Westminster Press, 1962).
9. C. S. Lewis, *Mere Christianity* (The Macmillan Company, 1952), p. vi.

10. C. S. Lewis, "Rejoinder to Dr. Pittenger," *The Christian Century*, Vol. LXXV (Nov. 26, 1958), p. 1360.

11. Lewis, *Mere Christianity*, p. vi.

12. C. S. Lewis, *Transposition and Other Addresses* (London: Geoffrey Bles, Ltd., 1949), p. 51.

13. C. S. Lewis, Preface to *The Incarnation of the Word of God*, by St. Athanasius (The Macmillan Company, 1946), p. 9.

14. C. S. Lewis, *The Problem of Pain* (London: Geoffrey Bles, Ltd., 1940; New York: The Macmillan Company, 1943), p. viii. Quotations from this work are reprinted by permission of Geoffrey Bles, Ltd., and The Macmillan Company.

15. C. S. Lewis, *Surprised by Joy: The Shape of My Early Life* (London: Geoffrey Bles, Ltd., 1955), p. 24.

16. *Ibid.*

17. *Ibid.*, p. 71.

18. *Ibid.*, p. 168.

19. *Ibid.*, p. 171.

20. *Ibid.*, p. 188.

21. *Ibid.*, p. 215.

22. *Ibid.*, p. 223.

23. C. S. Lewis *et al.*, *Essays Presented to Charles Williams* (London: Oxford University Press, 1947), p. xiv.

II. *The Apologetic Scene*

1. C. S. Lewis, *That Hideous Strength* (London: The Bodley Head, Ltd., 1945; New York: The Macmillan Company, 1946), p. 285 (Collier Books). Quotations from this work are reprinted by permission of The Bodley Head, Ltd., and The Macmillan Company. Copyright 1946 by C. S. Lewis.

2. C. S. Lewis, *The Voyage of the Dawn Treader* (London: Geoffrey Bles, Ltd., 1952; New York: The Macmillan Company, 1952), p. 175. Quotations from this work are reprinted by permission of Geoffrey Bles, Ltd., and The Macmillan Company. Copyright 1952 by The Macmillan Company.

3. Lewis, *Hideous Strength*, p. 307.

4. *Ibid.*, p. 293.

NOTES 209

5. C. S. Lewis, *They Asked for a Paper* (London: Geoffrey Bles, Ltd., 1962), p. 17.
6. *Ibid.*, p. 19.
7. *Ibid.*, p. 14.
8. *Ibid.*, p. 163.
9. Lewis, *Joy*, p. 196.
10. C. S. Lewis, *The Screwtape Letters* (London: Geoffrey Bles, Ltd., 1942; New York: The Macmillan Company, 1943), p. 140. Quotations from this work are reprinted by permission of Geoffrey Bles, Ltd., and The Macmillan Company.
11. *Ibid.*, p. 140.
12. C. S. Lewis, *The Pilgrim's Regress* (London: Geoffrey Bles, Ltd., 1943; Grand Rapids, Michigan: Wm. B. Eerdmans Publishing Company, 1958), p. 36. Quotations from this work are reprinted by permission of Geoffrey Bles, Ltd., and Wm. B. Eerdmans Publishing Company.
13. C. S. Lewis, *Out of the Silent Planet* (London: The Bodley Head, Ltd., 1938; New York: The Macmillan Company, 1943), pp. 26–27 (Collier Books). Quotations from this work are reprinted by permission of The Bodley Head, Ltd., and The Macmillan Company.
14. C. S. Lewis, *Miracles: A Preliminary Study* (The Macmillan Company, 1947), p. 199.
15. Lewis, *Paper*, p. 162.
16. Julian Huxley, *Religion Without Revelation* (rev. ed.; Harper & Brothers, 1957), p. ix.
17. Lewis, *Hideous Strength*, pp. 70–71.
18. *Ibid.*, p. 41.
19. *Ibid.*, p. 42.
20. C. S. Lewis, *The Abolition of Man* (London: Geoffrey Bles, Ltd., 1946), p. 54.
21. Lewis, *Hideous Strength*, p. 42.
22. C. S. Lewis, *The Great Divorce: A Dream* (London: Geoffrey Bles, Ltd., 1945; New York: The Macmillan Company, 1946), p. 71. Quotations from this work are reprinted by permission of Geoffrey Bles, Ltd., and The Macmillan Com-

pany. Copyright 1946 by The Macmillan Company.

23. Lewis, *Hideous Strength*, p. 294.

24. Lewis, *Pilgrim's Regress*, p. 70.

25. C. S. Lewis, *Letters to Malcolm: Chiefly on Prayer* (Harcourt, Brace and World, Inc., 1964), p. 105.

26. Lewis, *Abolition*, p. 14.

27. Lewis, *Hideous Strength*, p. 353.

28. C. S. Lewis, Preface to *The Hierarchy of Heaven and Earth: A New Diagram of Man in the Universe*, by D. E. Harding (Harper & Brothers, 1953), p. 10.

29. C. S. Lewis, *The World's Last Night and Other Essays* (Harcourt, Brace and World, Inc., 1960), pp. 56–57.

30. Lewis, *Transposition*, p. 35.

31. Lewis, *Hideous Strength*, p. 185.

32. *Ibid.*, p. 23.

33. Lewis, *Transposition*, p. 39.

34. Lewis, *Hideous Strength*, p. 37.

35. Lewis, *Paper*, pp. 139–149.

36. Lewis, *Hideous Strength*, p. 130.

37. Lewis, *Paper*, p. 20.

38. Lewis, *Malcolm*, p. 152.

39. *Ibid.*

40. Lewis, *Miracles*, p. 113.

41. Lewis, *Mere Christianity*, p. 21.

42. C. S. Lewis, "Difficulties in Presenting the Christian Faith to Modern Unbelievers," *Lumen Vitae*, Vol. III (Sept., 1948), pp. 424–425.

43. Kilby, *op. cit.*, p. 180.

III. *The Foundation of Apologetics*

1. C. S. Lewis, *Rehabilitations and Other Essays* (Oxford University Press, Inc., 1939), p. 157.

2. In *Rehabilitations*.

3. See especially *The Personal Heresy, The Allegory of Love*, and *Studies in Words*.

4. C. S. Lewis, *Studies in Words* (Cambridge University Press, 1960), p. 6.

5. C. S. Lewis, *The Allegory of Love: A Study in Medieval Tradition* (Oxford University Press, Inc., 1936), p. 44.

6. Eustace M. W. Tillyard and C. S. Lewis, *The Personal Heresy: A Controversy* (Oxford University Press, Inc., 1939), p. 111.

7. C. S. Lewis, "A Sacred Poem: Review of *Taliessin Through Logres*," by Charles Williams, *Theology*, Vol. XXXVIII (April, 1939), p. 270.

8. Lewis, *Allegory*, p. 47.

9. *Ibid.*, p. 48.

10. C. S. Lewis, ed., *George Macdonald: An Anthology* (The Macmillan Company, 1947), p. 21.

11. C. S. Lewis, *Perelandra* (London: The Bodley Head, Ltd., 1938; New York: The Macmillan Company, 1946), p. 144 (Collier Books). Quotations from this work are reprinted by permission of The Bodley Head, Ltd., and The Macmillan Company. Copyright 1944 by C. S. Lewis.

12. *Ibid.*, p. 201.

13. Lewis, *Allegory*, p. 60.

14. Lewis, *Rehabilitations*, p. 154.

15. *Ibid.*, p. 157.

16. Lewis, *Screwtape*, pp. 11–12.

17. Lewis, *Divorce*, p. 41.

18. Lewis, *Hideous Strength*, p. 72.

19. Lewis, *Abolition*, p. 36.

20. Lewis, *Miracles*, p. 38.

21. Lewis, *Hideous Strength*, p. 138.

22. Lewis, *Mere Christianity*, p. 108.

23. Lewis, *Paper*, p. 185. See "On Obstinacy in Belief," pp. 183–196.

24. Lewis, *Screwtape*, p. 47.

25. Lewis, *Paper*, p. 196.

26. *Ibid.*, pp. 166–182.

27. *Ibid.*, p. 175.

28. Lewis, *Miracles*, pp. 134–135.

29. Lewis, *Paper*, p. 177.

30. C. S. Lewis, *Reflections on the Psalms* (Harcourt, Brace

and World, Inc., 1958), pp. 99–108.

31. Lewis, *World's Last Night*, p. 97.
32. Lewis, *Psalms*, p. 116.
33. *Ibid.*
34. *Ibid.*, p. 112.
35. *Ibid.*, p. 114.
36. Lewis, *World's Last Night*, p. 99.
37. Rudolf Bultmann *et al.*, *Kerygma and Myth: A Theological Debate*, ed. by Hans Werner Bartsch (rev. Harper Torchbook ed.; Harper & Row, Publishers, Inc., 1961), p. 10.
38. Lewis, *Miracles*, p. 161n.
39. Lewis, *Pain*, p. 64.
40. Lewis, *Paper*, p. 158.
41. Lewis, *Miracles*, p. 161n.
42. Lewis, *Paper*, p. 156.
43. *Ibid.*, p. 161.
44. Lewis, *Miracles*, p. 96.
45. Lewis, *Malcolm*, p. 74.
46. Lewis, *Mere Christianity*, p. 135.
47. Lewis, *Miracles*, p. 99.
48. It is true that Lewis' early writings more heavily stressed the transcendence of God. But that was because he thought the then present situation demanded it. However, transcendence and immanence were always balanced in his thinking and were more explicitly balanced in his later writings, e.g., in *Letters to Malcolm*. Lewis defends himself against the charge of quasi deism in his "Rejoinder to Dr. Pittenger," *loc. cit.*
49. Lewis, *Malcolm*, p. 106.
50. *Ibid.*, p. 34.
51. Lewis, *Pain*, p. 16.
52. *Ibid.*, p. 23.
53. *Ibid.*, p. 35.
54. Lewis, *Miracles*, p. 107.
55. Lewis, *Malcolm*, p. 120.
56. Book IV of *Mere Christianity* is entitled "Beyond Personality: Or First Steps in the Doctrine of the Trinity."

57. Lewis admits that "there is a passage in my *Problem of Pain* which would imply, if pressed, a shockingly crude conception of the Incarnation." ("Rejoinder to Dr. Pittenger," *loc cit.*, p. 1359.) Lewis corrected the passage in the French edition. But that passage is not representative of his thought.
58. Lewis, *Mere Christianity*, p. 140.
59. *Ibid.*, p. 41.
60. Lewis, *Miracles*, p. 136.
61. Lewis, *Malcolm*, p. 96.
62. Lewis, *Mere Christianity*, p. 45.
63. Lewis, *World's Last Night*, p. 100.
64. Lewis, *Pain*, p. 67.
65. *Ibid.*, p. 64.
66. *Ibid.*, p. 71.
67. *Ibid.*, pp. 54–55.
68. Lewis' most detailed discussion of salvation is in *Mere Christianity*, pp. 134–175, which forms the basis for much of the above synopsis.
69. Lewis, *Transposition*, p. 37.
70. Lewis, *Pilgrim's Regress*, p. 155.
71. Lewis, *Malcolm*, p. 134.
72. *Ibid.*, p. 133.
73. Lewis, *Mere Christianity*, p. 80.
74. Lewis, *Abolition*, p. 33.
75. Lewis, *Pain*, p. 53.
76. Lewis, *Malcolm*, p. 29.
77. Lewis, *Screwtape*, p. 112.
78. Lewis, *Malcolm*, p. 117.
79. Lewis, *Pain*, p. 103.
80. Lewis, *Divorce*, p. 67.
81. *Ibid.*, p. 64.
82. *Ibid.*, p. 113.
83. *Ibid.*, p. 72.
84. Lewis, *Pain*, p. 116.
85. See his essay "The Weight of Glory," in *Paper*, pp. 197–211.

86. C. S. Lewis, *The Last Battle* (The Macmillan Company, 1956), p. 161.
87. Lewis, *Paper*, p. 208.
88. Lewis, *Malcolm*, p. 140.
89. N. W. Clerk (pseud. of C. S. Lewis), *A Grief Observed* (The Seabury Press, Inc., 1963), p. 35.
90. Lewis, *Malcolm*, p. 158.
91. Lewis, *World's Last Night*, p. 107.
92. *Ibid.* See his essay "The World's Last Night," pp. 93–113.
93. John Wain, "Pleasure, Controversy, Scholarship," Review of *English Literature in the Sixteenth Century Excluding Drama, The Spectator*, Vol. CXCIII (Oct. 1, 1954), p. 403.
94. Lewis, *Rehabilitations*, p. 184.
95. C. S. Lewis, *An Experiment in Criticism* (Cambridge University Press, 1961), p. 141.
96. *Ibid.*, p. 132.
97. *Ibid.*, pp. 135–136.
98. *Ibid.*, p. 137.
99. Lewis, *Hideous Strength*, p. 33.
100. Lewis, *Personal Heresy*, p. 119.
101. *Ibid.*, p. 120.
102. Lewis, *Rehabilitations*, p. 195.
103. Lewis, *Studies in Words*, p. 6.
104. C. S. Lewis, Letter to the Editor, *The Christian Century*, Vol. LXXV (Dec. 31, 1958), p. 1515.
105. *Ibid.*
106. Cooke, *loc. cit.*
107. E. G. Lee, *C. S. Lewis and Some Modern Theologians* (London: Lindsey Press, 1944), p. 12.
108. E. L. Allen, "The Theology of C. S. Lewis," *The Modern Churchman*, Vol. XXXIV (Jan.–March, 1945), pp. 317–318.
109. Lewis, "Rejoinder to Dr. Pittenger," *loc. cit.*
110. *Ibid.*, p. 1361.

IV. The Apologetic Method

1. J. V. Langmead Casserley, *op. cit.*, pp. 141–142.
2. C. S. Lewis, "Hedonics," *Time and Tide*, Vol. XXVI (June 16, 1945), p. 495.
3. Lewis, *Macdonald*, pp. 16–17.
4. Lewis, *Criticism*, p. 46.
5. Lewis, "On Stories," *Essays to Williams*, p. 98.
6. Lewis, *Perelandra*, p. 45.
7. *Ibid.*, p. 47.
8. C. S. Lewis, "The Gods Return to Earth," Review of *The Fellowship of the Ring*, by J. R. R. Tolkien, *Time and Tide*, Vol. XXXV (Aug. 14, 1954), p. 1082.
9. Lewis, *Perelandra*, p. 144.
10. *Ibid.*, p. 147.
11. Charles Moorman, *Arthurian Triptych: Mythic Materials in Charles Williams, C. S. Lewis, and T. S. Eliot* (University of California Press, 1960), discusses the Arthurian elements in Lewis' writings.
12. Lewis, *Silent Planet*, pp. 153–154.
13. C. S. Lewis, *Till We Have Faces: A Myth Retold* (London: Geoffrey Bles, Ltd., 1956), Introduction.
14. *Ibid.*, p. 305.
15. Lewis, *Criticism*, p. 72.
16. *Ibid.*, p. 45.
17. *Ibid.*, p. 49. By "literary" Lewis does not mean merely "educated," but rather the capacity to surrender oneself to the author's mind and to enter into his opinions.
18. C. S. Lewis, *The Magician's Nephew* (The Macmillan Company, 1955), p. 103.
19. *Ibid.*, p. 112.
20. Roger L. Green, *Tellers of Tales* (rev. ed.; London: E. Edmund Ward [Publishers] Ltd., 1953), p. 259.
21. Charles A. Brady, "Finding God in Narnia," *America*, Vol. XCVI (Oct. 27, 1956), p. 103.
22. C. S. Lewis, *The Silver Chair* (London: Geoffrey Bles, Ltd., 1953; New York: The Macmillan Company, 1953), p. 17.

Quotations from this work are reprinted by permission of Geoffrey Bles, Ltd., and The Macmillan Company. Copyright 1953 by The Macmillan Company.

23. Roger L. Green, *C. S. Lewis* (Henry Z. Walck, Inc., Publishers, 1963), p. 49.
24. Brady, *loc. cit.*, p. 104.
25. Lewis, "On Stories," *Essays to Williams*, p. 100.
26. Quoted in Green, *C. S. Lewis*, p. 38.
27. Lewis, *Dawn Treader*, p. 209.
28. Lewis, *Allegory*, p. 44.
29. *Ibid.*, p. 113.
30. *Ibid.*, p. 47.
31. Lewis, *Pilgrim's Regress*, p. 5.
32. Leonard Bacon, Review of *The Screwtape Letters*, *Saturday Review*, Vol. XXVI (April 17, 1943), p. 20.
33. Lewis, *Screwtape*, Preface.
34. *Ibid.*
35. *Ibid.*
36. *Ibid.*
37. Lewis, *Divorce*, p. 8.
38. *Ibid.*, p. 64.
39. *Ibid.*, p. 116.
40. Churchill, *loc. cit.*, p. 339.
41. Lewis, *Mere Christianity*, p. 33.
42. Charles Hartshorne, "Philosophy and Orthodoxy: Reflections Upon C. S. Lewis' *The Problem of Pain* and *The Case for Christianity*," Ethics, Vol. LIV (July, 1944), p. 295.
43. Lewis, *Pain*, p. 14.
44. *Ibid.*, p. 76.
45. Lewis, *Miracles*, p. 15.
46. *Ibid.*, p. 72.
47. *Ibid.*, p. 97.
48. *Ibid.*, p. 162.
49. Horton Davies, *Varieties of English Preaching, 1900–1960* (Prentice-Hall, Inc., 1963), p. 190.
50. Lewis, *Malcolm*, p. 99.

51. Lewis, *Pilgrim's Regress*, p. 37.
52. Lewis, *Mere Christianity*, p. 31.
53. C. S. Lewis, "Bulverism," *Time and Tide*, Vol. XXII (March 29, 1941), p. 261.
54. Lewis, *Paper*, p. 188.
55. Lewis, *Hideous Strength*, p. 115.
56. Lewis, *Malcolm*, p. 154.
57. Lewis, *Divorce*, p. 40.
58. Lewis, *Miracles*, p. 198.
59. Lewis, *Pilgrim's Regress*, pp. 151–152.
60. Lewis, *Miracles*, p. 155.
61. Lewis, *Paper*, p. 163.
62. Lewis, *Silent Planet*, pp. 135–136.
63. Lewis, *Hideous Strength*, p. 296.
64. *Ibid.*, p. 371.
65. Sydney J. Harris, "Shafts from a Christian Marksman," Review of *The World's Last Night*, *Saturday Review*, Vol. XLIII (March 5, 1960), p. 22.
66. David Elton Trueblood, *Philosophy of Religion* (Harper & Brothers, 1957), p. 107.
67. Lewis, *Pilgrim's Regress*, p. 10.
68. Lewis, *Mere Christianity*, p. 106.
69. Lewis, *Miracles*, p. 158.
70. Lewis, *Paper*, p. 165.
71. *Ibid.*, pp. 200–201.
72. Lewis, *Pain*, pp. 134–135.
73. Lewis, "Difficulties in Presenting the Christian Faith to Modern Unbelievers," *loc. cit.*, p. 425.
74. Lewis, *Silver Chair*, pp. 153–155.
75. Lewis, *Mere Christianity*, p. 51.
76. Davies, *op. cit.*, p. 175.
77. Lewis, *Malcolm*, p. 135.
78. Lewis, *Psalms*, p. 114.

BIBLIOGRAPHY

I. BOOKS BY C. S. LEWIS

A. Theology

The Abolition of Man: Or Reflections on Education with Special Reference to the Teaching of English in the Upper Forms of Schools. London: Oxford University Press, 1943. New edition, London: Geoffrey Bles, Ltd., 1946; New York: The Macmillan Company, 1947.

Beyond Personality. London: Geoffrey Bles, Ltd., 1944; New York: The Macmillan Company, 1945.

Broadcast Talks. London: Geoffrey Bles, Ltd., 1942; published as *The Case for Christianity,* New York: The Macmillan Company, 1942.

Christian Behaviour: A Further Series of Broadcast Talks. London: Geoffrey Bles, Ltd., 1943; New York: The Macmillan Company, 1943. *Christian Reflections.* Edited by Walter Hooper. Wm. B. Eerdmans Publishing Company, 1967.

The Four Loves. London: Geoffrey Bles, Ltd., 1960; New York: Harcourt, Brace and World, Inc., 1960.

(Ed., with a Preface). *George Macdonald: An Anthology.* London: Geoffrey Bles, Ltd., 1946; New York: The Macmillan Company, 1947.

The Great Divorce: A Dream. London: Geoffrey Bles, Ltd., 1946; New York: The Macmillan Company, 1946.

A Grief Observed. The Seabury Press, Inc., 1963. (Under the pseudonym of N. W. Clerk.)

Letters to Malcolm: Chiefly on Prayer. London: Geoffrey Bles, Ltd., 1964; New York: Harcourt, Brace and World, Inc., 1964.

Mere Christianity: A revised and enlarged edition, with a new introduction, of the three books The Case for Christianity, Christian Behaviour, and Beyond Personality. London: Geoffrey Bles, Ltd., 1952; New York: The Macmillan Company, 1952.

Miracles: A Preliminary Study. London: Geoffrey Bles, Ltd., 1947; New York: The Macmillan Company, 1947.

The Pilgrim's Regress: An Allegorical Apology for Christianity, Reason and Romanticism. Rev. ed., with a new Preface, London: Geoffrey Bles, Ltd., 1943; Grand Rapids, Mich.: Wm. B. Eerdmans Publishing Company, 1959.

The Problem of Pain. London: Geoffrey Bles, Ltd., 1940; New York: The Macmillan Company, 1943.

Reflections on the Psalms. London: Geoffrey Bles, Ltd., 1958; New York: Harcourt, Brace and World, Inc., 1958.

The Screwtape Letters. London: Geoffrey Bles, Ltd., 1942; New York: The Macmillan Company, 1943. With "Screwtape Proposes a Toast" and a new Preface, London: Geoffrey Bles, Ltd., 1961; New York: The Macmillan Company, 1961.

Surprised by Joy: The Shape of My Early Life. London: Geoffrey Bles, Ltd., 1955; New York: Harcourt, Brace and World, Inc., 1956.

They Asked for a Paper. London: Geoffrey Bles, Ltd., 1962.

Till We Have Faces: A Myth Retold. London: Geoffrey Bles, Ltd., 1956; New York: Harcourt, Brace and World, Inc., 1957.

Transposition and Other Addresses. London: Geoffrey Bles, Ltd., 1949. Published as *The Weight of Glory and Other Addresses,* New York: The Macmillan Company, 1949.

The World's Last Night and Other Essays. Harcourt, Brace and World, Inc., 1960.

B. Space Novels

Out of the Silent Planet. London: The Bodley Head, Ltd., 1938; New York: The Macmillan Company, 1943; New York: Collier Books, 1962.

Perelandra. London: The Bodley Head, Ltd., 1943; New York: The Macmillan Company, 1946; New York: Collier Books, 1962.

That Hideous Strength: A Modern Fairy-Tale for Grown-ups. London: The Bodley Head, Ltd., 1945; New York: The Macmillan Company, 1946; New York: Collier Books, 1962.

C. Children's Novels

The Horse and His Boy. London: Geoffrey Bles, Ltd., 1954; New York: The Macmillan Company, 1954. Rev. ed., The Macmillan Company, 1962.

The Last Battle. London: The Bodley Head, Ltd., 1956; New York: The Macmillan Company, 1956. Rev. ed., The Macmillan Company, 1962.

The Lion, the Witch and the Wardrobe. London: Geoffrey Bles, Ltd., 1950; New York: The Macmillan Company, 1950.

The Magician's Nephew. London: The Bodley Head, Ltd., 1955; New York: The Macmillan Company, 1955. Rev. ed., The Macmillan Company, 1962.

Prince Caspian: The Return to Narnia. London: Geoffrey Bles, Ltd., 1951; New York: The Macmillan Company, 1951. Rev. ed., The Macmillan Company, 1962.

The Silver Chair. London: Geoffrey Bles, Ltd., 1953; New York: The Macmillan Company, 1953. Rev. ed., The Macmillan Company, 1962.

The Voyage of the Dawn Treader. London: Geoffrey Bles, Ltd., 1952; New York: The Macmillan Company, 1952.

D. Literary Criticism

The Allegory of Love: A Study in Medieval Tradition. London and New York: Oxford University Press, 1936. (Also available in Galaxy paperback edition.)

(With Charles Williams). *Arthurian Torso: Containing the Posthumous Fragment of the Figure of Arthur by Charles Williams and a Commentary on the Arthurian Poems of Charles Williams by C. S. Lewis.* London and New York: Oxford University Press, 1948.

The Discarded Image: An Introduction to Medieval and Renaissance Literature. London and New York: Cambridge University Press, 1963.

English Literature in the Sixteenth Century Excluding Drama. (The Oxford History of English Literature, Vol. III.) London and New York: Oxford University Press, 1954.

An Experiment in Criticism. London and New York: Cambridge University Press, 1961.

(With E. M. W. Tillyard). *The Personal Heresy: A Controversy.* London and New York: Oxford University Press, 1939. (Also available in paperback. London and New York: Oxford University Press, 1965.)

A Preface to Paradise Lost. Revised and enlarged edition. London and New York: Oxford University Press, 1942. (Also available in Galaxy paperback edition.)

Rehabilitations and Other Essays. London and New York: Oxford University Press, 1939.

Studies in Medieval and Renaissance Literature. London and New York: Cambridge University Press, 1966.

Studies in Words. London and New York: Cambridge University Press, 1960.

E. Undefined

Dymer. New edition with a new Preface. New York: The Macmillan Company, 1950.

Poems. Edited by Walter Hooper. London: Geoffrey Bles, Ltd., 1964.

Spirits in Bondage: A Cycle of Lyrics. London: William Heinemann, Ltd., 1919. (Under the pseudonym of Clive Hamilton.)

II. Selected Writings on C. S. Lewis

Carnell, C. S., "The Dialectic of Desire: C. S. Lewis' Interpretation of Sehnsucht." Unpublished Ph.D. thesis, University of Florida, 1960.

Green, Roger Lancelyn, *C. S. Lewis*. Henry Z. Walck, Inc., Publishers, 1963.

Hart, Dabney, " C. S. Lewis's Defense of Poesie." Unpublished Ph.D. thesis, University of Wisconsin, 1959.

Kilby, Clyde S., *The Christian World of C. S. Lewis*. Wm. B. Eerdmans Publishing Company, 1964.

Moorman, Charles, *Arthurian Triptych: Mythical Material in Charles Williams, C. S. Lewis, and T. S. Eliot*. University of California Press, 1960.

Reilly, Robert J., " Romantic Religion in the Work of Owen Barfield, C. S. Lewis, Charles Williams, and J. R. R. Tolkien." Unpublished Ph.D. thesis, Michigan State University, 1960.

Walsh, Chad, *C. S. Lewis: Apostle to the Skeptics*. The Macmillan Company, 1949.

Wright, Marjorie E., " The Cosmic Kingdom of Myth in the Myth-Philosophy of Charles Williams, C. S. Lewis, and J. R. R. Tolkien." Unpublished Ph.D. thesis, University of Illinois, 1960.

www.ingramcontent.com/pod-product-compliance
Lightning Source LLC
Chambersburg PA
CBHW070315230426
43663CB00011B/2139